S. HRG. 113–168

VA CLAIMS SYSTEM: REVIEW OF VA'S TRANSFORMATION PROGRESS

HEARING

BEFORE THE

COMMITTEE ON VETERANS' AFFAIRS UNITED STATES SENATE

ONE HUNDRED THIRTEENTH CONGRESS

FIRST SESSION

DECEMBER 11, 2013

Printed for the use of the Committee on Veterans' Affairs

Available via the World Wide Web: http://www.fdsys.gov

U.S. GOVERNMENT PRINTING OFFICE

86–132 PDF   WASHINGTON : 2014

For sale by the Superintendent of Documents, U.S. Government Printing Office
Internet: bookstore.gpo.gov   Phone: toll free (866) 512–1800; DC area (202) 512–1800
Fax: (202) 512–2104   Mail: Stop IDCC, Washington, DC 20402–0001

CONTENTS

VA CLAIMS SYSTEM: REVIEW OF VA'S TRANSFORMATION PROGRESS

WEDNESDAY, DECEMBER 11, 2013

U.S. SENATE,
COMMITTEE ON VETERANS' AFFAIRS,
Washington, DC.

The Committee met, pursuant to notice, at 10:03 a.m., in room 418, Russell Senate Office Building, Hon. Bernard Sanders, Chairman of the Committee, presiding.

Present: Senators Sanders, Murray, Brown, Begich, Blumenthal, Burr, Isakson, Boozman, and Heller.

OPENING STATEMENT OF HON. BERNARD SANDERS, CHAIRMAN, U.S. SENATOR FROM VERMONT

Chairman SANDERS. Good morning. Thanks, everybody, for coming to what I believe will be a very informative and important hearing on an issue that is of concern to veterans all over this country and to every Member of this Committee.

Today, we are going to continue our oversight of VA's efforts to transform the claims system. As members will recall, earlier this year this Committee met to discuss one of the major challenges confronting VA, the claims backlog.

I think all of us have heard from veterans who are deeply concerned about the backlog. It is a concern to the Veterans Service Organizations, I know it is a concern to every Member of this Committee, and I suspect every member of the Senate.

The origin of this problem goes back a number of years. It has everything, in my view, to do with the reality that, until 2008—and maybe at some point General Hickey can give me some clues about this—for whatever reason, there was no serious effort on the part of VA to do what every other major corporation and government agency in this country had done, and that is, move from the world of paper to electronics.

I do not quite understand, given the enormous amount of paper facing VA historically, why it took so long for them to do that. Nonetheless, that was the case.

Furthermore, VA has also had to deal with a staggering number of new claims, tragically, for veterans who served in Afghanistan and Iraq. On top of that, VA—I think appropriately—made sure that veterans who were impacted by Agent Orange in Vietnam also got the benefits to which they were determined to be eligible for. So, that is a lot of stuff coming in.

Nonetheless, this Committee, at our hearing in mid-March, despite all of these factors, heard about the unacceptably large number of claims that were pending and the numerous challenges confronting VA. It is my view, and I believe it is the view of every Member of this Committee, that no veteran in our country should have to wait years to have his or her claim adjudicated. It is a disgrace and that is an issue that must be dealt with.

Today, as I understand it, VA is going to give us some good news, welcome news, about significant progress made in this area. When we last met in March to discuss this issue, there were over 896,000 claims in the inventory. Of that number, more than 632,000 or 70 percent were backlogged or pending longer than VA's goal of 125 days. That is a staggering number.

Today, as I understand it, those numbers look much different and, in fact, are much improved. The number of claims pending longer than 125 days, or officially part of the backlog, has dropped to just over 395,000 claims or 57 percent of the total inventory. That is still a large number but is a significant improvement. The total number of pending claims has dropped to its lowest level since July 2012 at slightly less than 694,000 claims.

Let me be clear—and I think we can all agree on this—many challenges remain. This Committee will touch on some of those challenges and I will deal with them in my statement this morning.

We must, however, begin today by acknowledging the progress we have seen since we last met in March. I want to thank General Hickey and her staff and maybe most importantly, the hundreds and thousands of hard-working folks at VA all over this country who have put their shoulder to the wheel to see the improvements that we are going to be talking about today. So, I want to thank VA for those improvements.

For the fourth year in a row, VA has processed more than one million claims. This is no small feat given the sheer size of the transformation the Department is undertaking.

VA is moving to an electronic claims processing system and VBMS, which is a major component of that system, has been deployed to every regional office, as I understand it, ahead of schedule.

The Department has implemented a new organizational model changing the way in which it processes claims, and it continues to build upon efforts to improve employee training and address underperforming regional offices. I believe this Committee has worked in a productive and bi-partisan manner to support VA's efforts while also holding it accountable for meeting its ambitious claims processing goals. I have said this before and I say it again.

I applaud General Shinseki, Secretary of VA, for having the courage to do what I think very few public officials do. He put in black and white a goal, so there is no ambiguity attached to it. He said that he wants to see all claims processed within 125 days at 98 percent accuracy by 2015.

So, he has put VA out on a line on this issue, and we will be talking with General Hickey and the others today to see, in fact, whether they are on schedule to achieve that goal. That is very clearly an extremely ambitious goal.

Following the March hearing, I was joined by all of my colleagues on this Committee in asking for DOD's, the Department of Defense's, continued commitment to help VA eliminate the backlog. That is a huge issue, and we have got to move forward on this.

This Committee continues to closely monitor, and when necessary, encourage greater cooperation between the Departments because at the end of the day this problem is not going to be solved until there is greater cooperation.

Members from both sides of the aisle have presented legislative ideas to address these problems. I am confident a number of these ideas, including significant portions of the Claims Processing Improvement Act that I introduced earlier this year, will pass the Senate this week as part of a veteran's omnibus bill. So, we are making some legislative progress in this area.

This Committee also continues to conduct aggressive oversight of VA's transformation efforts, in part through hearings like this one, in order to hold VA accountable for meeting its ambitious claims processing goals.

Despite the very good progress that I think we are going to hear about today, we all know—I do not think there is any debate on this—that VA is not yet where it needs to be in addressing the very serious problem of the backlog issue.

Veterans are still waiting too long for a decision and the Inspector General continues to find issues with the quality of the work.

I am concerned by the most recent IG findings, which found significant problems with provisional rating decisions reviewed at the Los Angeles Regional Office, and this is an issue we will want to discuss this morning.

During Committee oversight, my staff has identified clear and unmistakable errors in provisional rating decisions. I am pleased to hear VA is taking action to remedy the problems identified by the IG.

However, this should have been done immediately upon recognition of the problem at the local level; and here I think is the important point that I want to make.

Reducing the backlog at the expense of accuracy is not acceptable. Our goal is to move forward rapidly to make sure that this backlog goes down but we will not do it at the expense of accuracy.

This Committee will continue to examine the oldest claims first initiative and the issuance of provisional rating decisions. This is an enormously important issue.

The Committee's oversight efforts will also continue to focus on other components of transformation to ensure VA is providing timely and accurate decisions.

For example, VA still has a long way to go in creating a truly electronic claims processing system, a system that does not rely on the scanning of millions of pieces of paper.

VA must also ensure that, as it transitions to a Web-based system, it does not inadvertently disadvantage certain populations of claimants, such as elderly veterans or those veterans living in rural areas, with limited internet access. A very important issue in States like Vermont.

Finally, VA must do more to address other work pending at the ROs, regional offices, such as appeals and award adjustments. Despite the significant reduction in claims measured as part of the backlog, other pending work has continued to climb since our last hearing on this issue.

Finally, let me touch on a few areas that I believe VA needs to focus on in its efforts to transform the claims system. VA must focus on the appellate process. This is a large part of the claims system, and it is not receiving, in my view, the attention that it deserves.

General Hickey, I know VA has been piloting a number of ideas in the Houston Regional Office, but I think we need some increased leadership attention on these efforts in order to ensure real progress is being made on appeals.

In that regard, the numbers are not good. According to VA's Performance and Accountability Report, last year it took on average 866 days, as I understand it, to provide a final decision on an appeal.

Let me repeat that. Veterans were waiting on average 866 days for a final decision on an appeal. This is why providing an accurate initial decision, by the way, is so important, so we do not have to go through the appeals process.

General Hickey, I am requesting of you today to get back to us as soon as you possibly can, certainly if you can by the end of January, with how you plan to improve the processing of the appellate workload at the ROs.

In 2009, VA began an effort to revise and update VA's rating schedule which is an enormously complicated process, and I know and I think we are all aware that this is painstaking work, but I am concerned about the progress of this effort.

In the fall of 2012, the GAO provided a comprehensive review of this effort and the associated challenges. The rating schedule is the foundation of the claims system and any future updates will impact every piece of transformation from the rules based calculators to employee training. VA will need to spend significant time and energy reprogramming computers, modifying forms and ensuring employees are properly trained on the updated schedule.

As VA moves forward with this update, it must plan accordingly. Too often in the past, the Department was not prepared to cope with major changes to the claims system and that failure resulted in negative experiences for veterans. Let us not see history repeat itself in that area.

Finally, VA needs to continue to demonstrate with data and hard facts how transformation will ultimately improve the veteran experience and result in more timely and accurate decisions.

In closing, let me say this. I am pleased by the fact that VA has taken very seriously the claims backlog. General Hickey and her staff are working very, very hard to address this problem. It is very clear that significant progress has been made, and we appreciate that very much. But it is also clear that a whole lot of important work remains to be done.

So, we appreciative that General Hickey is with us today. We are going to begin speaking with her in a moment.

First, Senator Burr is not yet here and Senator Isakson will be acting as ranking member.

Senator Isakson.

STATEMENT OF HON. JOHNNY ISAKSON, U.S. SENATOR FROM GEORGIA

Senator ISAKSON. Thank you, Mr. Chairman. I would like to welcome the members of VA for sharing their testimony today. We appreciate them coming.

As we will hear today, VA has taken a number of steps to try to improve its handling of disability claims and, in recent months, the backlog has started to decline. Although any true progress is welcome, I think there are still many reasons for concern.

To start with, nearly 700,000 veterans and their families do not yet have an answer to their requests for benefits, and they can expect to wait at least 9 months for a decision. Also, we continue to hear from veterans' groups about how often VA makes mistakes in the processing disability claims.

In fact, The American Legion recently testified that it found errors in over half of the decisions that it reviewed last year. This is of real concern to me and to every Member of the Committee because it can take years for a veteran to correct those errors through VA's appeal process.

Today, more than a quarter of a million appeals are waiting to be resolved. This number has been trending upward, not downward. The work has also been piling up, such as claims, for accrued benefits, responses to incoming mail, and adjustments to monthly checks based on how many dependents a veteran is claiming.

The number of dependency adjustments waiting for VA decision has tripled in just over 2 years, and what VA calls the "correspondence" has grown nearly five times since last year.

All of this raises questions about VA and its prioritization work that is not counting the backlog statistic.

Mr. Chairman, I want to follow up on your comments with regard to provision problems that we have seen. As you know, the Committee asked the Inspector General to review the provisional initiative to make sure claimants would receive appropriate, quality decisions without any unnecessary hurdles.

Although that review is not finished, the Inspector General testified last week that it found 10 errors out of 11 provisional decisions at one regional office.

In fact, it appears that the employees were encouraged to violate VA policy by making provisional decisions without first obtaining necessary medical examinations. That office has now reviewed all of its provisional decisions and found hundreds that contained errors.

Mr. Chairman, all of this suggests that more must be done to make sure VA's efforts to reduce the backlog will not cause veterans and their families more delays or more frustrations down the road.

VA must be held accountable for making real, lasting improvements in the services provided to those seeking benefits from VA which they have earned. I look forward to working with you and the rest of the Committee to ensure that happens.

I thank the Chairman.

Chairman SANDERS. Thank you, Senator Isakson.

Senator Murray.

STATEMENT OF HON. PATTY MURRAY,
U.S. SENATOR FROM WASHINGTON

Senator MURRAY. Thank you very much, Mr. Chairman. I really do appreciate your holding this hearing.

Ending this claims backlog and building a timely, accurate claims processing system is one of the absolute top priorities for our veterans. I continue to hear frequently from veterans in my homestate of Washington that they are still waiting far too long for their claims to be completed. I know that getting this right is a top priority for the Department and I understand this is a very complex problem that has no single, easy solution.

So, I am encouraged by the steps VA has taken so far, but we have a very long way to go.

VA's initiative to expedite the oldest claims was a good step. However, I have heard repeatedly from veterans that they were confused and frustrated with the provisional rating process. Some believe their claims have been flat out rejected and others did not understand that they had a year to submit additional evidence.

Under Secretary Hickey, we need to hear more from you today about how VA is going to improve outreach and communication with veterans so that future initiatives do not cause so much confusion on the ground.

While the numbers are moving in the right direction, we need to know that the necessary structural changes, as the Chairman referenced, are being made as well. This is especially important in handling the more complex claims.

The recent testimony by the office of the Inspector General shows some of the examples of these problems. It is not surprising these claims take longer to rate. These are also claims for veterans who need their benefits the most and we need to keep that in mind.

So, as VA continues to work to bring the backlog down, we cannot prevent them from doing their jobs either. That means keeping the government open. The entirely unnecessary shutdown of the government forced us into some very bad circumstances earlier this year. VA had to furlough 7,800 the VBA employees. They ended mandatory overtime for our claims processors; and as Secretary Shinseki testified, it decreased claims production by an average of 1,400 claims every day.

So all of you know, Chairman Ryan and I announced our budget agreement last night. I cannot stress enough how important it is for everyone to help us pass this agreement so that we can get away from governing by crisis and presenting another government shutdown in January and protecting our veterans as we did in the past from serious harm that we saw in October.

So, I look forward to continuing to work with all of our colleagues, with you, Under Secretary Hickey, and meeting the challenges that we have.

Mr. Chairman, thank you for having this really critical hearing.

Chairman SANDERS. Well, Senator Murray, thank you and thank you for your work on the budget process.

Senator Heller.

STATEMENT OF HON. DEAN HELLER,
U.S. SENATOR FROM NEVADA

Senator HELLER. Mr. Chairman, thank you and to the Ranking Member, thank you also for holding this hearing.

An issue that I do not think is lost on anybody is about the critical mission facing the Veterans Benefits Administration. I think every person in this room knows the seriousness of this problem, but I specifically want to underscore how this is affecting veterans in Nevada.

4,000 veterans in Reno, Las Vegas, and across Nevada are waiting for VA target deadline of 125 days for their claim to be completed. They are waiting more than 125 days. On average, veterans wait 436 days to have their claims completed, which is the longest wait of any regional office in the Nation. I think we can all agree that this is unacceptable.

I know for a fact that, Under Secretary Hickey, you are committed to fixing this issue, and I appreciate you recognizing the gravity of this problem. I want to thank you personally for your staff working with mine in trying to look for better ways to handling these issues.

I also want to thank you for working with Senator Brown's staff also as we try to come together with ideas to see if we can bring this problem to an end.

It is important to me and my constituents to bring this one particular story to your attention. A Las Vegas veteran wrote me recently, "I am just one more disabled veteran still fighting the appeals process with the VA. I understand now that no one is going to expedite my appeal, and I will probably die before I get any successful resolution. But there are a huge number of vets just like me and some in worse shape. None of us deserve to be put on hold forever."

Frustration. That is what this veteran and veterans across the Nation are feeling. I, as well as my colleagues, want this to be fixed for the good of our veterans. There is no doubt about that, and I am proud to have teamed up with some of my colleagues to thoroughly examine the claims process front to back and from every perspective.

The reality is that VA has a 1945 process. This outdated process no longer makes sense for VA nor for the veteran. Looking back at two decades of VA backlog, I have found that VA has always fixed the problem with short-term solutions rather than asking the difficult question of whether the entire process needs to be updated.

VA needs a 21st-century benefit delivery system for our Nation's veterans but there is not going to be one silver bullet, I think we can all agree, that solves this particular problem.

It is going to take multiple proposals that address multiple aspects of the claims process for us to really reach a resolution but that means it is time for all stakeholders to open up about what needs to be fixed and how to fix it.

VA has a role to play. Veterans Service Organizations and the Congress have a role to play. Even the veterans themselves have a part to play in resolving this. It no longer makes sense to point fingers and to place blame as we have for quite sometime now. Instead, Congress needs to meet and give VA and the regional offices the tools and resources they need to bring the backlog down but this cannot be done without an open, frank discussion about what is working and what is not.

Congress needs to work together with VA and the VSOs to solve this problem and solve it permanently so that this Committee is not back here in a few years having the same discussion.

I know the Chairman and Ranking Member are committed to that and I will be reaching out to them with solutions or about solutions that I have identified.

Our Nation owes it to veterans to resolve this problem and together keep our promises to care for them when they return home from war.

Thank you again, Under Secretary Hickey, for being here to testify. I want to thank everybody on the panel today for taking time for being here. I look forward to hearing about the progress VA has made in working with you, the VSOs, and the veterans, of course, to end this backlog.

Thank you.

Chairman SANDERS. Thank you, Senator Heller.

Senator Brown.

STATEMENT OF HON. SHERROD BROWN, U.S. SENATOR FROM OHIO

Senator BROWN. Thank you, Mr. Chairman, I will be very brief.

General, thank you for joining us. It is good to see you again and I appreciate your public service as well as all of the panel.

I appreciate the VBA transformation plan. I think the results you outlined in your testimony are admirable and important and positive. I echo Senator Heller and others on this Committee that this has obviously got to improve. You know that. We will not lecture you on that.

I will bring up in the question period something that I still do not quite understand. The average claim has been pending, according to VA's Monday Morning Report this week, the average claim nationally is 167 days.

In Cleveland it is 208 days. It has persistently been the highest second-highest, or third-highest in the country. We have not really had good answers for that. I guess I want to know less about why than will it be fixed.

167 days, obviously, is way too long. Another 40 days on top of that is something that we need to work on. So, I appreciate the work you are doing and look forward to figuring this out.

Thank you.

Chairman SANDERS. Thank you, Senator Brown.

Senator Boozman.

STATEMENT OF HON. JOHN BOOZMAN, U.S. SENATOR FROM ARKANSAS

Senator BOOZMAN. Thank you, Chairman and Ranking Member Burr, for having this hearing. In the interest of time, let us move on and I look forward to hearing the testimony of the panel.

Chairman SANDERS. Thank you very much.

Senator Begich.

STATEMENT OF HON. MARK BEGICH,
U.S. SENATOR FROM ALASKA

Senator BEGICH. Thank you very much, Mr. Chairman. I apologize that I will not be able to stay that long but I do want to make a few comments.

Under Secretary Hickey, thank you and I thank VA for the improvements. I know there have been, since I have been here, back and forth and you have suffered through many meetings here on this side as well as the other side.

I do want to say at least in the Alaska region things are improving and we want to recognize that and give you credit for that plus the hard work I know the employees there are doing. They are under a lot of stress and I know when the shutdown occurred it added more.

So, I appreciate the work you are doing, but I just want to highlight for the record and also to give you a sense that even though we are making improvements there are still some challenges; and give you some specific cases that in a lot of ways it is easy to find the specific cases because our office usually gets those calls very quickly. I will give you just a couple that I want to kind of bring to your attention.

For example, one vet that came in who was 100 percent disabled under SSDI but only 20 percent under VA because of their coding process, the VA's coding process, had not been completed or updated to address the artificial discs replacement in his back. A simple little thing, yet pretty significant for that individual who was trying just to get something done.

Or in the situation—because they contacted us and we moved very quickly—the vet and his wife who literally cried on the phone when they got their permanent total disability claim reviewed and approved literally overnight, and the reason was because the PTD finding allowed enrollment for the CHAMPVA allowing his wife to be able to enroll so she could get the necessary insurance for brain cancer that she was dealing with and was able to ensure that she was no longer at risk or at least limited risk of disability.

Or the vet who was found 100 percent disabled with a mental health condition who was living in a six-by-eight room without windows in a basement before we got his claim expedited and approved.

Then the vet who was waiting a year to get adjustments to their pension for adding a dependent, that is, that they got married.

The vet whose lung cancer is attributable to Agent Orange exposure but the COPD attributable to the lung cancer is not considered service-connected.

Why I bring those up is because we then work at the constituent end in trying to solve these problems. The way we will judge the success and I will judge success of what work you are doing is when we are not making these calls because they are being processed without having us to make those calls.

Those examples are sometimes extreme but real and it really puts a face on these individuals where sometimes we are in these meetings and we talk a lot about data and statistics and days and so forth. But really when it boils down to it, they are individuals who are experiencing in their life the most important thing or could be the most extreme situation.

So, I do want to echo the concern we have in trying to get these numbers down and the timeline, but also I want to credit your folks for the improvement over the last 4 or 5 years and the priority you have placed on this.

We know it is not just VA. We know DOD is part of this equation, and you have been partnered or your agency as well as DOD have had several meetings where we have put some pressure on them. It may have been in this Committee or in the Appropriations Committee, trying to get this moving forward because it is not just on your back but predominantly and significantly you have a huge role once it is in your hands.

So, I again want to commend you for the work but also recognize that there is still a lot more to do I appreciate your giving me a chance to talk about these Alaskans who everyday, you know—it is probably the largest input we get, from veterans contacting us about their concerns and obviously disability claims is one of those.

So, I thank you. I apologize that I will not be able to be here for the questions and the testimony but I know our staff is working aggressively with you. And again, your Alaska team is working double-time and we know that and we are going to keep some pressure on them, as you can imagine.

So, thank you very much.

Chairman SANDERS. Thank you Senator Begich.

Senator Blumenthal.

STATEMENT OF HON. RICHARD BLUMENTHAL, U.S. SENATOR FROM CONNECTICUT

Senator BLUMENTHAL. Thank you, Mr. Chairman, and thank you for having this hearing.

First of all, General Hickey, thank you for the work that you and VA are doing. I know that General Shinseki is personally committed to eliminating the backlog.

I met with him, in fact, in Connecticut and had an opportunity to talk to him about this subject. So, nothing we say here is to imply that this backlog is the result of any sort of malevolence or personal animus on the part of anybody at VA. We are all grappling with a common challenge here but there is still a lot of work to be done to reach the goal of 98 percent accuracy and an end to the backlog by 2015.

Just a few quick points. Accuracy is important. We do not want to sacrifice accuracy for the sake of eliminating the backlog because accuracy is itself a source of problems if it is ignored. So, I cannot emphasize strongly enough how timing and deadlines are important but accuracy matters to the person on the ground.

To take one example, Michael Scovetta, a veteran who served our country in Iraq and Afghanistan, was denied his application after a 2-year wait; and he has now been waiting a full year for his appeal. Obviously, the 2-year wait was regrettable but the potential inaccuracy of his denial is also important.

I want to thank Senator Murray for her work to avoid another shutdown because in another case the shutdown itself aggravated the timing issue. Jordan Massa, an Iraq and Afghanistan veteran who received a Purple Heart, had to wait for 2 years for his application to be approved but then waited another month due to the government shut down.

So, the point here is that different issues, challenges, problems are interconnected and interrelated. Just to finish on this point of talking about interrelated problems, electronic medical records.

The Chairman has mentioned it in his opening remarks. I have talked about it, I think, almost every opportunity in this room at every hearing, and I want to commend VA for its willingness to move forward, its interest in resolving these issues.

I again express regret that the Department of Defense apparently has been less cooperative than VA, but one way or the other this problem has to get solved so that these records are truly interoperable, so that the system is seamless.

There is no reason for someone leaving active duty as a member of our United States military and then becoming "a veteran," should not have been the benefit of completely seamless electronic medical records. And I am going to pursue legislation.

I know the Chairman has expressed his concern and other Members of the Committee are committed as well.

So, thank you for your work on this issue. As much as we seem critical, and we are, we are also supportive because we have a common goal.

Thank you, Mr. Chairman.

Chairman SANDERS. Thank you, Senator Blumenthal.

I would now like to welcome General Allison Hickey, the Undersecretary for Benefits at VA.

General Hickey, thank you for joining us today to address the Department's progress in eliminating the claims backlog and what you are going to do to address the remaining very serious problems.

We are interested in an update on the transformation currently underway and the successes and challenges presented by this effort.

General Hickey is accompanied by Diana Rubens, the Associate Deputy Under Secretary for Field Operations; Brad Houston, the Director of VBA's Office of Business Process Integration; and Richard Hipolit, an Assistant General Counsel in VA's Office of General Counsel.

We thank you all very much for being here.

General Hickey, please begin.

STATEMENT OF HON. ALLISON A. HICKEY, UNDER SECRETARY FOR BENEFITS, U.S. DEPARTMENT OF VETERANS AFFAIRS; ACCOMPANIED BY DIANA M. RUBENS, ASSOCIATE DEPUTY UNDER SECRETARY FOR FIELD OPERATIONS, VETERANS BENEFITS ADMINISTRATION; BRAD HOUSTON, DIRECTOR, OFFICE OF BUSINESS PROCESS INTEGRATION, VETERANS BENEFITS ADMINISTRATION; AND RICHARD HIPOLIT, ASSISTANT GENERAL COUNSEL, OFFICE OF GENERAL COUNSEL

Ms. HICKEY. Thank you. Good morning, Chairman Sanders, Ranking Member Burr, and Members of the Committee. Thank you for the opportunity to update you on the Veterans Benefits Administration's transformation efforts and progress we have made to date.

In recent months, VA has made significant progress in executing our Benefit Claims Transformation Plan. We reduced the backlog impacting our veterans by approximately 36 percent since March of this year, and we expect these reductions to continue over the next year.

More importantly, while our employees have increased their productivity, they have also increased the quality of their work at the same time.

In June 2011, when I arrived, our average for claims accuracy was approximately 83 percent; as of the end of November 2013, the number was approximately 90 percent at the claim level. When measuring accuracy at the medical issue level, which is a more precise measure of VA's quality, our rating accuracy today stands at nearly 97 percent. So, in other words, we have done more and better for our veterans, their families, and survivors.

That said, we continue to push closer to the Secretary's goal of completing our veterans claims in 125 days at 98 percent accuracy in 2015. Our veterans deserve no less from us.

None of this progress would be possible were it not for the tremendous support VA receives from its partners. This Committee and the Congress's sustained support for VBA's budget and legislative requirements over the last 4 years has fostered significant headway for implementation of our plan and enabled VBA to complete a record one million claims for 4 consecutive years.

Our Veterans Service Organizations and labor partners and those at the Federal, State, and local level have worked in close collaboration with us throughout this transformation to roll out new initiatives and provide the best possible service to our veterans, their family members, and survivors.

Our progress would not be possible without the support of our partners in VA Office of Information and Technology who continue to work tirelessly to deliver new capabilities to improve productivity and workload management; our Veterans Health Administration partners who co-located physicians within our regional office workforce to provide on-site support for medical opinions and expedited claim examination at unprecedented levels; our IRS and Social Security partners who now provide us data every week; and our DOD partners who are collaborating more and more to deliver the new gold standard service treatment and personnel records and other capabilities.

Finally, but most importantly, this progress would not be possible without the exceptionally committed tremendous effort and dedication of VBA's employees—52 percent of these are veterans themselves; the majority of others are direct family members of a veteran.

They have each worked tirelessly in mandatory overtime for the last 8 months serving veterans, their families, and survivors by working an additional 20 hours every month for those 8 months. Many employees continue to work overtime in voluntary status even now.

Let me highlight some key outcome statistics as of December 7 that show our progress: inventory, down from a peak of 884,000 to

693,000 or 191,000 claims down, 22 percent reduced; backlog, down from a peak of 611,000 in March 2013 to 395,000, a decrease of 216,000 or 36 percent. Nearly one-third of the backlog is gone.

Claim level accuracy increased from approximately 83 percent in 2011 to 90 percent today.

Medical issue accuracy is approximate 97 percent today. We cut our B2, or exam errors, by 50 percent across the Nation by focusing on them hard this year. We trained over 3,500 employees through the new challenge training where they rate claims 150 percent faster and are 30 percent more accurate at the end of the training.

We have completed more than 45,000 reviews by our quality review teams to catch errors earlier in the process before a final outcome for the veteran, avoiding those errors in the outcomes.

We have completed 1.17 million claims in fiscal year 2013, an all-time historic high for VBA and 4 months of record-breaking production.

We completed 99.9 percent of all claims older than 2 years; 67,000 veterans waiting the longest now have a quality decision. We completed over 96 percent of all claims in the 1-year-old category from 513,000 veterans in April of this year to approximately 18,000 that remain.

We have already completed 61 percent of all claims older than 334 days, our next tranche. We will continue to drive the age of these claims down until we hit 125 and, and 98 percent quality in 2015.

You can see it for yourself in our Monday Morning Workload Report where our pending workload today is, on average, 100 days younger than it was this time last year.

We have also fully implemented one of our people initiatives, our new Transformational Organizational Model in all 56 regional offices 9 months ahead of schedule and are seeing a 10 percent increase in production as we predicted in the plan.

We built the Stakeholder Enterprise Portal and granted 1,148 credentials to our VSO partners, representing over 75 organizations. We are currently building and testing the capability to connect digit-to-digits with their electronic claims submission systems, as well.

We grew our fully-develop claims receipts from 3 to 27 percent since February because of our great partnerships with our VSOs. We are even seeing some VSOs take the fully develop claims issue to new levels providing even the Federal records and exams completed in a disability benefit questionnaire, or DBQ, making these claims ready to rate.

We have VHA physicians in our regional offices now providing just-in-time medical opinions, DBQs, acceptable clinical evidence or ACE exams, and simple time-saving, quick on-the-spot answers to raters who need clarification.

We have supported over 3.2 million active accounts in eBenefits up from 250,000 in June 2011 and now eBenefits hosts 50 self-service features including over the last year the ability to file a claim online, upload your own evidence, and submit your claim directly into a VBMS. When I last spoke to you, we had received a total of 1,500 claims this way. Today, we receive 1,000 a week this way.

We deployed VBMS to every regional office, medical center, records management center, appeals management center a full 6 months ahead of schedule. Under the original VBMS transformation plan, we would still be delivering VBMS to regional offices for the first time this month.

Instead, we have more than 25,000 users and have converted more than 360 million images from paper into digital format at a 99 percent quality level.

We have created or converted 75 percent of our current claims in the inventory into the digital format for processing electronically in the new VBMS system.

We have established the Newark Regional Office as a model for an electronic regional office or eRO, to test and validate the changes associated with converting to a completely paperless operation so we see no surprises.

Despite these recent outcome metrics and success, please know this, Mr. Chairman and Members of this Committee, we still recognize that many veterans wait too long to receive the benefits that they have earned and deserved. This has never been acceptable to VA and it remains unacceptable to VA.

No one in VBA is "taking a knee" as we would have said in our military careers and the combined effects of our transformation plan are having a positive impact for many of our veterans, their families, and survivors.

I thank this Committee for your continued support especially as we move into our crucial fiscal year—2014.

[The prepared statement of Ms. Hickey follows:]

PREPARED STATEMENT OF ALLISON A. HICKEY, UNDER SECRETARY FOR BENEFITS, VETERANS BENEFITS ADMINISTRATION (VBA), U.S. DEPARTMENT OF VETERANS AFFAIRS (VA)

Good morning, Chairman Sanders, Ranking Member Burr, and Members of the Committee. Thank you for the opportunity to discuss VA's benefits claims processing transformation efforts. I am accompanied today by Richard Hipolit, Assistant General Counsel, Brad Houston, Director of VBA's Office of Business Process Integration, and Diana Rubens, VBA's Deputy Under Secretary for Field Operations.

In recent months, VA has made significant progress in executing our benefit claims Transformation Plan. We reduced the backlog by approximately 36 percent since March of this year, and we expect these reductions to continue over the next year. More importantly, while increasing our productivity, we have also increased the quality of our work. In June 2011, when I arrived, our average for claims accuracy was approximately 83 percent; as of the end of November 2013, that number was approximately 90 percent. When measuring accuracy at the medical issue level—which is a more precise measure of VA's workload—our rating accuracy today stands at 97 percent. My testimony today will focus on how execution of our Transformation Plan has decreased the backlog and increased quality, resulting in better service to the Veteran community and pushing us closer to the Secretary's goal of all claims completed in 125 days at 98-percent accuracy in 2015.

None of this progress would be possible were it not for the tremendous support VA receives from its partners. The direct support of this Committee and the Congress has helped us make significant headway on our Transformation Plan and enabled us to complete a record-breaking 1 million claims for 4 consecutive years. Our Veterans Service Organization (VSO) partners have worked in close collaboration with us throughout this transformation to roll out new initiatives and provide the best service possible to our Veterans, their family members, and Survivors. Our State Departments of Veterans Affairs partners across the country have helped us reduce the backlog at a local level by contributing resources to innovative Federal/state solutions. Our progress would not be possible without the support of our partners in the VA Office of Information and Technology, who continue to work tirelessly to deliver new capabilities to improve productivity and workload management, and our Veterans Health Administration (VHA) partners, who co-located physicians with our regional office workforce to provide onsite support for medical opinions and expedited claim examinations at unprecedented levels. Finally, this progress would not be possible without the tremendous effort and dedication of VBA's claims processing employees, who worked mandatory overtime for 6 months straight on this important mission.

VBA TRANSFORMATION PLAN: RESULTS THROUGH NOVEMBER 30, 2013

Here are some key statistics that show our progress:
- *Inventory:* Down from peak of 884,000 in July 2012 to 693,000—a decrease of 191,000 or 22 percent
- *Backlog:* Down from peak of 611,000 in March 2013 to 392,000—a decrease of 219,000 or 36 percent
- *"1-Year Claims" Initiative:* Approximately 96 percent complete from 513,000 in April 2013 to 20,000
- *Claim-Level Accuracy (12-month):* Increased from approximately 83 percent in 2011 to 90 percent today
- *Medical-Issue Accuracy (3-month):* Approximately 97 percent
- Completed 1.17 million claims in Fiscal Year (FY) 2013—an all-time high Completed 128,000 claims in August and 129,000 in September—an all-time high
- Recognized the 1 millionth GI Bill recipient in November 2013; approximately 82 percent of supplemental claims are now either fully or partially automated
- Granted 1,148 credentials to VSOs to use Stakeholder Enterprise Portal
- Approximately 75 percent of current claims in the inventory are in digital format for processing electronically within the Veterans Benefits Management System
- Converted more than 360 million images from paper into digital format
- Supporting over 3.2 million active accounts in eBenefits

Despite these recent successes, many Veterans still wait too long to receive benefits they have earned and deserve. This has never been acceptable to VA or to the dedicated employees of VBA—approximately 52 percent of whom are Veterans themselves. As this Committee knows from our previous discussions, VA's Transformation Plan includes initiatives to re-train and reorganize our people, streamline our business processes, and build and implement new technology solutions that are getting us out of paper-bound, manual processes to improve our service to Veterans, their families, and Survivors. There is no silver bullet in this Transformation Plan; the results being reported today cannot be attributed to any one single initiative or program but rather the collective synergy of all of them. However, I would like to take this time to review a few key initiatives that have had a significant impact on our increased production and quality and show promise for the way ahead.

VBA ORGANIZATIONAL MODEL

Initially planned for deployment throughout FY 2013, VBA accelerated the implementation of its new organizational model by 9 months due to early indications of its positive impact on performance. The new organizational model incorporates a case-management approach to claims processing, by reorganizing the workforce into cross-functional teams that give employees visibility of the entire processing cycle of a Veteran's claim. These cross-functional teams work together on one of three segmented lanes: express, special operations, or core. Lanes were created based on the complexity and priority of the claims, and employees are assigned to the lanes based on their experience and skill levels. An Intake Processing Center serves as a formalized triage process to quickly and accurately route Veterans' claims to the right lane when first received.

The Express Lane was developed to identify those claims with a limited number of medical conditions (i.e., about 1–2 issues) and subject matter which could be developed and rated more quickly. The Special Operations Lane applies intense focus and case management on specific categories of claims that require special processing or training (e.g., homeless or terminally-ill Veterans, military sexual trauma, former prisoners of war, seriously injured, etc.). The Core Lane includes claims with three or more medical issues that do not involve special populations of Veterans. Less complex claims move quickly through the system in the Express Lane, and the quality of our decisions improves by assigning more experienced and skilled employees to the more complex claims in our Special Operations Lane.

Thus far, we have seen a 10-percent increase in production in regional offices using the new model during the first 60 days of deployment. We have also seen processing speed in our Express Lanes improve; about 30 percent of claims are routed through Express Lanes and are being processed about 100 days faster than claims routed through Special Operations Lanes (approximately 10 percent of claims) or the Core Lanes (approximately 60 percent of claims).

VETERANS BENEFITS MANAGEMENT SYSTEM (VBMS)

VBMS, VA's Web-based electronic claims processing solution, was fully deployed to all 56 regional offices 6 months ahead of schedule in June 2013. Since then, VBA has also successfully deployed VBMS to the Appeals Management Center, the Records Management Center, the Board of Veterans' Appeals, all National Call Centers, and all VA medical centers. This new technology helps us get out of paper and begin reaping gains in processing speed within a digital claims processing environment; currently, more than 75 percent of our existing claims inventory is electronic and will be processed electronically. In addition, VBMS improves access, drives automation, and enables greater exchange of information and increased transparency to Veterans, our workforce, and our stakeholders.

The evolution of VBMS is occurring across four distinct generations of development. Generation One of VBMS began in 2010 with the conceptualization, piloting, development, and deployment of baseline system functionality with improved quality and efficiency. The development of Generation One of VBMS concluded with the successful implementation of Release 4.1 in January 2013.

As we moved into the development of Generation Two of VBMS, the focus has been on building additional system capabilities while leveraging simple automation features. VBA has deployed three major Generation Two software releases: VBMS 4.2, 5.0, and 5.1. These releases included improvements to correspondence and work queue tools, additional rating functionality, and more extensive data exchange and system integration capabilities.

VBMS 6.0, scheduled for release this month, will enhance existing features, integrate additional correspondence functionality, deliver initial capabilities to the Board of Veterans' Appeals, and add new functionality to allow claims processors to electronically request and receive service treatment records from the Department of Defense (DOD) Healthcare Artifacts and Image Management Solution (HAIMS).

Generation Three of VBMS, which will deploy in 2014, will increase system functionality, add more complex automation capabilities, and have the capability to accept Veterans' electronic service treatment records and personnel records from DOD. Additional workload management capabilities will also allow VBA to move claims electronically across regional office boundaries when needed. A national work queue is being developed based on this capability, which will route claims automatically based on VBA's priorities and essentially match a claims processor with the "next best claim" to work based on their skill level and national policy. All of these improvements will enable VBMS end-users, which include VA Medical Center personnel and VSOs, to perform their work more efficiently and accurately.

Enhancements to system capabilities in 2014 will increase both the production and quality of our claims decisions. In this year, VA will also have an additional opportunity to assess and validate the effectiveness of the model as a whole and implement improvements as needed.

Generation Four of VBMS, which will deploy in 2015, will capitalize on efficiencies and quality improvements gained during the previous year. VA will utilize enhancements made in Generation Three to identify additional automation and process improvement opportunities that can be incorporated into Generation Four, allowing employees to focus on more difficult claims by reducing the time required to process less complex claims.

VBA established the Veterans Claims Intake Program (VCIP) in 2012 to streamline the process for receiving records and data into VBMS and other VBA systems. VCIP converts claims and other paper records that we receive into a digital format that is usable within VBMS. Under VCIP, documents are scanned and converted into electronic format, and important information and data are extracted and populated in an electronic folder accessible to claims processors through VBMS. In November 2013, VCIP achieved a major milestone by surpassing 350 million images converted from paper and uploaded into VBMS.

EBENEFITS AND THE STAKEHOLDER ENTERPRISE PORTAL (SEP)

eBenefits is a joint VA/DOD client services portal that provides life-long engagement with Servicemembers, Veterans, and their families. VA has been strongly encouraging the use of eBenefits since October 2009, and just recently crossed the three-million-user mark. eBenefits users have access to more than 50 self-service features and greater access to benefits and health information at the time and method of their choosing. Through self-service, eBenefits users have generated over 370,000 requests for official military personnel documents, 379,000 requests for VA guaranteed home loan certificates of eligibility, approximately 29.1 million claim status requests, and over 3.2 million self-service letters. VA will continue to add more functionality and features to the site, with the goal of using it to anticipate Veterans' needs, prompt them when they're eligible for new benefits and services, and ultimately reach out to them instead of waiting until they reach out to us.

The integration of eBenefits with VBMS also enables Veterans to submit claims online. Using the Veterans On-line Application (VONAPP) Direct Connect (VDC) application in eBenefits, Veterans can file a claim online by answering a series of questions (which may seem familiar to users of today's tax preparation software like Turbo Tax), upload all their evidence and supporting documents, check the status of their claims, and much more. The electronic claims submission capability provided by VDC improves the timeliness of claims processing by leaping over the entire paper-based mail, triage, and claims establishment process. Claims filed in eBenefits feed right into VBMS, giving employees the ability to work these claims without ever having to touch a piece of paper. Today, VA receives about 1,000 claims each week through VDC. We are grateful for the support of all our partners—in the Congress, at the state and national VSO level, and in every State Department of Veterans Affairs across the country—for encouraging Veterans to use eBenefits and submit their claims electronically, which boosts productivity and helps us eliminate the backlog. VA distributed toolkits with information on eBenefits and fully developed claims (FDCs) to every Congressional office. eBenefits prompts Veterans to file FDCs when they submit a claim online and outlines the advantages in terms of improved decision timeliness. We ask that you continue to partner with us on promoting these important initiatives to Veterans in your states by adding information to your Web pages and in correspondence to constituents who are Veterans.

The third component of our online engagement strategy is the Stakeholder Enterprise Portal (SEP), which is a secure, Web-based connection that complements eBenefits and gives VSOs and other authorized advocates access to assist Veterans in filing disability claims electronically. Using the portal, VSOs can check the status of claims, review payment history, and upload documentation on behalf of the Veterans they represent—all within a digital environment. When filing a claim online in eBenefits, a Veteran can request the assistance of a VSO by choosing from a list of accredited representatives in VA's database. When logging into SEP, the chosen VSO representative is alerted to the Veteran's request, and upon acceptance, is given power-of-attorney authorization to access the Veteran's claim and assist with preparation. Once the VSO representative believes the claim is ready for submission, he or she can send notification back to the Veteran in eBenefits, and the Veteran submits the claim to VA. With SEP, 8,000 VSO representatives throughout the Nation can continue to perform their vital advocacy and assistance role within VA's transformed benefits delivery model. As of November 30, 2013, VA has registered more than 14 percent of all VSOs.

ELECTRONIC REGIONAL OFFICE (ERO)

On November 1, 2013, VBA established the Newark Regional Office as the first eRO. There are no longer any paper claims being processed at the Newark eRO. All claims are processed electronically, which allows us to refine, test, and streamline our operations as we prepare for a fully electronic environment nationwide. Veterans, Survivors, and families served by the Newark eRO do not experience any change in the way they interact with the Newark RO. Claims submitted in paper format continue to be accepted but are scanned and immediately entered into VBMS for electronic processing. We anticipate all 56 regional offices will be in a fully electronic environment later this year. Modeling the eRO at the Newark RO will enable us to understand the impacts on our current operations and help to ensure we have planned for a smooth transition. We continue to encourage all Veterans to file claims electronically through eBenefits and to utilize Veterans service organizations to assist them with their claims.

FULLY-DEVELOPED CLAIMS (FDC)

VA's FDC program is a critical tool for transforming the way we do business. The longest phase of the current claims-processing timeline is the phase in which VBA employees gather evidence. FDCs drastically reduce the length of this phase by allowing Veterans to submit claims as "fully developed," which means the claim includes all available supporting evidence like private treatment records, a notice of any other records held in Federal facilities, and a certification that the Veteran has no more evidence to submit. Veterans are not at any risk when submitting an FDC, because if we find that there is another piece of relevant evidence that is needed for a rating decision, our employees will work to obtain it on the Veteran's behalf and continue processing the claim.

The Congress and our state and VSO partners have been instrumental in helping us increase awareness and understanding of our FDC program, especially by supporting the FDC workshops we have conducted across the country. As a result of these efforts and many others, the use of FDCs has dramatically improved since last year. In the third quarter of FY 2012, VA received approximately 3.6 percent of all claims as FDCs; in the fourth quarter of FY 2013, we received almost 25 percent of all claims as FDCs. FDCs are currently processed in less than half of the time it takes to process non-FDCs.

CHALLENGE TRAINING AND QUALITY REVIEW TEAMS (QRTS)

VBA is committed to providing high quality, timely, and relevant training for both new and experienced personnel to ensure that claims quality continues to improve. To this end, our transformation efforts include redesigned programs and tools that standardize training for the disability compensation and pension benefit programs across our 56 regional offices.

VBA instituted national-level Challenge Training in 2011 and Quality Review Teams (QRTs) in 2012 to improve employee training and decision accuracy while decreasing rework time. Challenge Training is focused on building the overall skills and readiness of the workforce through an 8-week curriculum, and QRTs focus on fixing the most common sources of error in the claims-processing cycle. To date, approximately 3,000 employees have graduated from our Challenge Training program, and an additional 484 employees have undergone Station Enhancement Training (SET), which is based on the Challenge model for new employees. In FY 2013, rating accuracy for claims completed in Challenge training was 95.5 percent.

Evidence shows that these training sessions are having a significant impact on accuracy, timeliness, and production. Challenge graduates decide approximately 150 percent more claims per day than their predecessor cohorts, at 30-percent better accuracy. Before Challenge Training, employees processed about half a claim a day at approximately 60-percent accuracy during the first 6 months following graduation; today, claims processors trained under the new Challenge program complete about 1.6 claims a day at approximately 94-percent accuracy within 6 weeks of graduation. In addition, when an entire regional office undergoes SET, accuracy improves by approximately 8 percent, and monthly production improves by approximately 27 percent.

In 2012, VBA reassigned 573 of our most skilled and experienced employees from their duties as claims processors to serve on QRTs. In FY 2013, these QRTs conducted more than 145,000 in-process reviews, preventing errors before they can impact the Veteran and providing specialized re-training to claims processors so these errors can be prevented in the future. QRTs made a particularly big impact on the most common types of errors this year.

In 2012, VBA found that almost 40 percent of claims rework errors across VBA were occurring in the medical examination phase (identified as "B2" errors). In April 2012, we launched the B2 Error Reduction Initiative and trained QRT Coaches to lead a Lean Six Sigma project at their regional offices to reduce B2 errors by approximately 50 percent. We made the investment—both by taking 573 employees off the line to serve on the QRTs and by training every QRT coach in Lean Six Sigma— and we are now seeing the results. In FY 2013, we reduced the B2 error rate by more than 40 percent across all of VBA, which means Veterans will not have to wait as long for a decision on their claims, and they will receive a high-quality decision.

VA currently uses a 3-month rolling average to track the impact of these initiatives, and others like them, on rating accuracy. These metrics are reported in AS-PIRE, the monthly Dashboard providing information on how VBA and regional offices are doing in relation to 2015 aspirational goals, and can be seen online (www.vba.va.gov/reports/) by anyone inside or outside of VA. In FY 2012, VA showed a 3-percent increase in national accuracy—from approximately 83 percent to 86 percent. In FY 2013, our 3-month accuracy at the claims level rose to approximately 90 percent, meeting the goal we set for ourselves this year. The accuracy outcome goals for the next 2 years are approximately 93 percent in FY 2014 and 98 percent in FY 2015.

It is important to recognize that under the existing quality review system, any one error on the claim, no matter how many medical conditions must be developed and evaluated, makes the entire claim in error—the claim is therefore counted as either 100 percent accurate or 100 percent in error, with no credit for anything in between. Medical issues are defined as individually evaluated medical conditions. Given that the average number of medical issues included in each claim for recently separated Servicemembers is now in the 12 to 16 range, we do not believe the current all-or-nothing measure reflects the actual level of decision accuracy achieved. When we measure the quality of claims based on the individual medical issues rated (i.e., "issue-based accuracy"), the accuracy of our decisions is at approximately 97 percent. This issue-based accuracy approach also affords VBA the opportunity to precisely target those medical issues where we make the most errors, at the individual employee level, and develop and direct training in a targeted manner.

COLLABORATIONS AND PARTNERSHIPS

VBA is relying more and more on partnerships with Federal, state and non-profit agencies to improve benefits delivery for Veterans. A key component of VBA's transformation is leveraging technology to interface with partners to securely exchange Veteran information needed to verify benefits eligibility. Over the past year, VBA has worked to develop these interfaces with the agencies below, and steady progress is being made.

Defense Department Service Treatment Records

DOD continues to strive to provide VA with 100 percent of separating Servicemembers' complete and certified Service Treatment Records. During the third week of November 2013, DOD achieved a 90-percent certification rate. VBA continues to work with DOD to transition to receiving all Service Treatment Records electronically. This will be accomplished via HAIMS to VBMS interface, which is scheduled for implementation effective January 1, 2014.

Internal Revenue Service (IRS) and Social Security Administration (SSA) Data Sharing

In February 2013, VA developed an expanded data-sharing initiative with IRS and SSA to streamline income verification for pension applicants. This initiative enabled VBA to eliminate an annual reporting surge of 150,000 actions and redirect significant resources to address the backlog of dependency and indemnity compensation (DIC) claims from Survivors. As a result, we have doubled our output of DIC claims processing with this effort, cutting the inventory in half and ensuring approximately 74 percent of all DIC claims are completed within 125 days.

VSOs and State and County Service Officers

Currently, VA's Digits-to-Digits (D2D) project allows VSOs, County Veterans representatives, and State Veterans Affairs agencies to directly submit electronic compensation claims into VA's digital claims system using their own existing systems. Allowing our partners this connectivity dramatically increases access to VA for Veterans and their advocates. We have already seen six claims management software providers build to VA's D2D specifications to make their products more competitive to their customer base of VSOs and County and State Veterans Affairs agencies. This path is very similar to the online tax preparation model provided by IRS, in which IRS published technology standards and specifications for how to send/receive data and then allowed the private sector to develop solutions for their customers to file their tax returns with IRS. While D2D is currently focused on digital submission of disability claims, this model can be extended to other benefits delivery programs in VA.

OLDEST CLAIMS INITIATIVE

On April 19, 2013, VBA began to implement a special initiative to quickly decide the oldest claims in the inventory. This initiative was created to accelerate the elimination of the backlog for Veterans who have waited the longest for a decision, and is a key part of VA's overall strategy to eliminate the claims backlog in 2015.

In June, VA completed the first phase of the initiative, which focused on all claims that had been pending over 2 years. While some claims from that category were still outstanding due to the unavailability of a claimant and other unique circumstances, approximately 99 percent of these 2-year claims (over 67,000) had been processed for Veterans, eliminating those claims from the backlog. Since that milestone, VBA claims processors have focused on completing the claims of Veterans who have been waiting over 1 year for a decision. VA has processed approximately 96 percent of all 513,000 claims pending over 1 year.

Several key factors have made this important initiative a success:

Veterans Health Administration (VHA) Collaboration. First, the contribution of our VHA partners has been critical. During this period, VHA physicians have been working in each of VBA's regional offices to provide onsite support for medical opinions, reducing deferral rates and increasing efficiency. They have been a key node in the management process by tracking those medical exams that are needed for rating decisions and ensuring the information is flowing between the administrations.

Mandatory Overtime. Mandatory overtime is a management tool that VBA implemented starting May 20, 2013, to maximize productivity during the oldest claim initiative. While in mandatory overtime, Rating Veterans Service Representatives (RVSRs), Veterans Service Representatives (VSRs), and Decision Review Officers (DROs) worked a minimum of 20 hours of overtime per month and focused exclusively on completing priority claims—claims over 1 year, FDCs, and special-interest claims (homeless, hardship, former prisoner of war, terminally ill, etc.). From May 20 to September 30, 2013, VBA's daily rating production increased over 30 percent, or more than 1,000 additional claims per day. VBA also recorded its highest monthly production rates ever in August and September 2013—over 128,000 and 129,000 respectively. Mandatory overtime was halted during the 2-week Government shutdown in October but was re-established and continued through November 23, 2013. VBA anticipates mandatory overtime to resume in 2014, contingent upon available funding. Optional overtime for claims processors will remain in effect.

National-level Workload Management. The oldest claims initiative also validated the need for a national approach to workload management. Historically VBA has maintained regional office claims processing jurisdictions that are aligned with state boundaries. This results in less-than-optimal utilization of VBA claims processing capacity. In recent years, VBA has "brokered" claims between regional offices via file transfer in order to maximize national claims processing resources. During VBA's focus on the oldest claims, more than 100,000 claims were brokered, ensuring the right "next claim" is matched with resources available nationwide. When the full system capacity is leveraged and state boundaries are disregarded, VBA achieves a much higher level of production.

The future state of VBA's brokering capabilities lies in the continued development of VBMS and a workload that is entirely electronic. The workload management capabilities of VBMS are being developed in two steps. Currently, a working group is building the design requirements that will provide managers with the tools and reporting capabilities to manage their workload most effectively at the regional office level. Second, a national work queue is being developed, to include the capability to route claims automatically through a pre-determined set of logic that matches claims processors with the "next best claim" to work, based on their skills and competencies and nationally set priorities.

Improved Production and Increased Accuracy. The results of our transformation efforts, including the oldest claims initiative, have proven that increased production does not have to come at the expense of decision quality. During this recent period of unprecedented production, VBA's 3-month rolling average for claims accuracy has steadily improved, from approximately 86 percent at the beginning of the year, increasing to 90 percent as of the end of November 2013. Issue-level accuracy has improved to approximately 97 percent. August 2013 proved to be the most productive month in VBA history for claims processing—with 128,594 claims completed—and in September our performance was even stronger, completing 129,488 claims.

CONCLUSION

While we know there is much more work to be done to reach our goals, the combined effects of our Transformation Plan—the people, process, and technology innovations and initiatives that have been developed and deployed—are having an impact. The gains we are making in information technology and the automation of our processes are critical, and going forward, we will need to sustain the resources for programs like VBMS in order to eliminate the backlog in 2015 and achieve our quality goals. Much of our success is attributable to the support of this Committee and your commitment to helping us in our transformation. I thank you for that—and for your full support of our information technology budgets. FY 2014 is a crucial year in our transformation, and I look forward to your continued support and commitment on behalf of Veterans, their families, and Survivors.

———

RESPONSE TO PREHEARING QUESTIONS SUBMITTED BY HON. RICHARD BURR TO U.S. DEPARTMENT OF VETERANS AFFAIRS

Question 1. In April 2013, VA announced an initiative to focus on claims that have been pending for at least one year, called its Oldest Claims First Initiative.

a. In total, how many claims were included in this initiative?

VBA Response: VBA's Oldest Claims First initiative included 512,942 claims. Through December 5, almost 495,000 of 512,942 of the oldest claims have been completed (96.5 percent), reducing the over-one-year claims remaining to be worked under this initiative to 18,005 (3.5 percent).

VBA previously submitted a response to this question that may have been confusing and only included information through September 30, 2013. The numbers above reflect information as of December 5, 2013.

b. Of those, how many claims have received a final decision and how many have received a provisional decision?

VBA Response: Through November 8, 2013, a total of 14,871 claims received a provisional rating, including 7,513 2-year claims and 7,358 1-year claims. This represents approximately two percent of the rating-related decisions made under the Oldest Claims Initiative through November 8, 2013. The use of provisional rating decisions ended on November 8, 2013.

c. Please provide redacted copies of at least ten provisional decisions that have been issued in connection with this initiative.

VBA Response: VA provided 10 copies of provisional decisions to the Committee on 12/09/2013. Due to file size, these were delivered on CD.

[Redacted submissions were received and are being held in Committee files.]

Question 2. According to the Monday Morning Workload Report, the number of items pending under End Product (EP) 400 (Correspondence) increased from less than 5,200 in September 2010 to over 70,500 in September 2013.

a. For the hearing record, please explain what work items are included under EP 400 and whether it includes claims that received provisional decisions under VA's Oldest Claims First Initiative.

VBA Response: Traditionally, VBA utilized the EP 400 to track correspondence actions that did not require a decision and only required a written response (e.g., a letter requesting the status of a claim).

In fiscal year 2011, VBA expanded the use of EP 400 to track two types of claims filed under the 2009 Agent Orange presumption policy change.

On April 19, 2013, VBA once again expanded its use of the EP 400 to track a subset of claims completed during the Oldest Claims Initiative. EP 400, with an additional tracking label, is used to identify claims that received a provisional rating decision for claimants who are both in receipt and not in receipt of VA benefits at the time of the decision.

b. Are any of the work items reflected under EP 400 included in VA's statistics on the backlog of claims that VA aims to eliminate by 2015?

VBA Response: EP 400 is not included in VA's statistics on the backlog of claims. VBA has defined the "backlog," as rating claims pending greater than 125 days. Rating claims are considered claims for disability compensation, dependency and indemnity compensation, and Veterans' pension benefits, including both original and supplemental claims. Rating claims generally require a disability rating decision by a Rating Veterans Service Representative.

Question 3. According to the Monday Morning Workload Report, the number of items pending under EP 930 (Review, including quality assurance) increased from less than 14,700 in September 2010 to over 26,500 in September 2013.

a. For the hearing record, please explain what work items are included under EP 930 and whether it includes claims that received provisional decisions under VA's Oldest Claims First Initiative.

VBA Response: Traditionally, EP 930 was used to track completed claims that subsequently require review, such as quality assurance reviews or award corrections. Because VA had already taken rating end-product credit on these claims, reviews or corrective actions are tracked in this "non-credit" series.

On April 19, 2013, VBA expanded its use of EP 930 to track a subset of claims completed during the Oldest Claims Initiative. EP 930, with a date of claim 364 days from the date of the provisional rating decision, identifies provisional rating decisions issued to claimants not in receipt of VA benefits at the time of the decision. This end product was established to ensure a final rating decision is issued to these claimants.

b. Are any of the work items reflected under EP 930 included in VA's statistics on the backlog of claims that VA aims to eliminate by 2015?

VBA Response: Actions pending under EP 930 are not included in VA's statistics on the backlog of claims. VBA has defined the "backlog" as rating claims pending greater than 125 days. Rating claims are considered claims for disability compensation, dependency and indemnity compensation, and Veterans' pension benefits, including both original and supplemental claims. Rating claims generally require a disability rating decision by a Rating Veterans Service Representative.

Question 4. According to the Monday Morning Workload Report, the number of items pending under EP 130 (Dependency) increased from less than 49,000 in September 2010 to over 210,000 in September 2013 and nearly 72 percent of those 210,000 work items have been pending for more than 125 days.

a. Please explain what work items are included under EP 130.

VBA Response: EP 130 applies to all actions involving dependency determinations, where the primary issue involves entitlement of the Veteran to increased benefits based on relationship or dependency.

b. During that time, has VA suspended work on these items or placed a lower priority on this work?

VBA Response: VBA completed a record number of non-rating claims in FY 2013 (875k), which includes EP 130 dependency claims. This is a 16% increase over FY12.

c. Are any of the work items reflected under EP 130 included in VA's statistics on the backlog of claims that VA aims to eliminate by 2015?

VBA Response: EP 130 is not included in VA's statistics on the backlog of claims. VBA has defined the "backlog," as rating claims pending greater than 125 days. Rating claims are considered claims for disability compensation, dependency and indemnity compensation, and Veterans' pension benefits, including both original and supplemental claims. Rating claims generally require a disability rating decision by a Rating Veterans Service Representative.

Question 5. According to the Monday Morning Workload Report, the number of items pending under EP 290 (Misc. determinations) increased from less than 27,000 in September 2010 to over 87,000 in September 2013 and 83 percent of those 87,000 work items have been pending for more than 125 days.

a. Please explain what work items are included under EP 290.

VBA Response: EP 290 applies to adjudicative decisions relating to eligibility benefits under other VA programs; programs of other Federal and State agencies; and independent determinations relating to elections, waivers, guardianship issues and other issues affecting payments. Examples of EP 290 work include adjustments due to incarcerations, claims for clothing allowance, and eligibility for loan guaranty benefits.

b. During that time, has VA suspended work on these items or placed a lower priority on this work?

VBA Response: VBA completed a record number of non-rating claims in FY 2013 (875k), which includes EP 290 claims. This is a 16% increase over FY12.

c. Are any of the work items reflected under EP 290 included in VA's statistics on the backlog of claims that VA aims to eliminate by 2015?

VBA Response: EP 290 is not included in VA's statistics on the backlog of claims. VBA has defined the "backlog," as rating claims pending greater than 125 days. Rating claims are considered claims for disability compensation, dependency and indemnity compensation, and Veterans' pension benefits, including both original and supplemental claims. Rating claims generally require a disability rating decision by a Rating Veterans Service Representative.

Question 6. According to the Monday Morning Workload Report, the number of items pending under EP 600 (Due process) increased from less than 20,000 in September 2010 to over 52,700 in September 2013 and 52 percent of those 52,700 work items have been pending for more than 125 days.

a. Please explain what work items are included under EP 600.

VBA Response: EP 600 can be used for two different types of VBA actions. Most often, EP 600 identifies cases where a predetermination notice is provided to a VBA beneficiary proposing to reduce benefits. EP 600 can also be applied to claims where VA proposes to find the claimant unfit to manage their VBA benefits.

b. During that time, has VA suspended work on these items or placed a lower priority on this work?

VBA Response: VBA completed a record number of non-rating claims in FY 2013 (875k), which includes EP 600 claims. This is a 16% increase over FY12.

c. Are any of the work items reflected under EP 600 included in VA's statistics on the backlog of claims that VA aims to eliminate by 2015?

VBA Response: EP 600 is not included in VA's statistics on the backlog of claims. VBA has defined the "backlog," as rating claims pending greater than 125 days. Rating claims are considered claims for disability compensation, dependency and indemnity compensation, and Veterans' pension benefits, including both original and supplemental claims. Rating claims generally require a disability rating decision by a Rating Veterans Service Representative.

Question 7. According to the Monday Morning Workload Report, the number of items pending under EP 165 (Accrued) increased from less than 3,700 in September 2010 to over 15,300 in September 2013.

a. Please explain the nature of the work items included under EP 165.

VBA Response: EP 165 applies to claims for compensation or pension payable as reimbursement of the expenses of last sickness and burial, or claims for accrued benefits payable based on relationship.

b. During that time, has VA suspended work on these items or placed a lower priority on this work?

VBA Response: VBA completed a record number of non-rating claims in FY 2013 (875k), which includes EP 165 claims. This is a 16% increase over FY12.

c. Are any of the work items reflected under EP 165 included in VA's statistics on the backlog of claims that VA aims to eliminate by 2015?

VBA Response: EP 165 is not included in VA's statistics on the backlog of claims. VBA has defined the "backlog," as rating claims pending greater than 125 days. Rating claims are considered claims for disability compensation, dependency and indemnity compensation, and Veterans' pension benefits, including both original and supplemental claims. Rating claims generally require a disability rating decision by a Rating Veterans Service Representative.

———

RESPONSE TO POSTHEARING QUESTIONS SUBMITTED BY HON. BERNARD SANDERS TO U.S. DEPARTMENT OF VETERANS AFFAIRS

Question 1. During the hearing Under Secretary Hickey testified that veterans were able to access VONAPP to file pension claims using a portal at the bottom of the Pension Home Page on VA's Internet site. However, according to the information on this site pension claims must be submitted in paper form. There is a link on the Pension Home Page to allow veterans to obtain and print out a pension application for paper submission. The page states: "This application will need to be completed and mailed to the appropriate VA Regional Office based on the state in which you reside."

Please clarify the ability of veterans to file pension claims on-line, including any timetable for restoration of on-line applications for pension claims in VONAPP, e-Benefits or any other portal.

Response. Veterans wishing to apply for pension do not currently have the capability to apply online. However, the application for pension remains available for download and printing through the VA pension Web site. While VA only received 30 pension claims per month through the VONAPP system, we agree that it is necessary to maintain some online capability in legacy systems during the transition to new systems. Therefore, VA is currently evaluating several options to restore the capability to submit an online application for pension. Since we are still evaluating options, we do not yet have a timetable for restoration. Additionally, as part of our transformation, we plan to deploy the pension application within eBenefits during fiscal year 2015.

Question 2. The Department's written testimony states: "In FY 2013, these QRTs conducted more than 145,000 in-process reviews, preventing errors before they can impact the Veteran and providing specialized re-training to claims processors so these errors can be prevented in the future. QRTs made a particularly big impact on the most common types of errors this year."

a. How are the errors identified by Quality Review Teams (QRT) tracked to capture the most common errors in order to better focus employee training?

Response. All errors identified by the QRTs are entered into the Automated Standardized Performance Elements Nationwide, the computer program used to track performance for the quality elements.

b. How many errors were identified during the more than 145,000 in-process reviews?

Response. A total of 16,651 errors were identified.

c. What were the three most common errors identified by the more than 145,000 in-process reviews?

Response. The three most common types of errors identified during the in-process reviews were:

• Rating the case without requesting an exam;
• Failure to request a medical opinion; and
• Rating a case based on an insufficient medical exam.

d. How to these errors compare to the most common errors identified by VA's Systematic Technical Accuracy Review and the most common reasons for remands issued by the Board of Veterans' Appeals?

Response. The errors noted on the in-process reviews are consistent with errors found in Systematic Technical Accuracy Reviews. The Veterans Benefits Administration does not currently have a way to compare these numbers to remands issued by the Board of Veterans' Appeals.

Question 3. The Department's written testimony states, "In 2012, VBA found that almost 40 percent of claims rework errors across VBA were occurring in the medical examination phase (identified as "B2" errors)."

a. How has training QRT coaches in Lean Six Sigma contributed to the reduction of B2 errors?

Response. For the period of November 2011 through October 2012, there were 624 B2 errors out of 2,274 total benefit entitlement errors (27.4 percent). For the period of November 2012 through October 2013, there were 344 B2 errors out of 1,687 total benefit entitlement errors (20.4 percent). This represents a 45 percent reduction in the number of B2 errors since the inception of QRTs in 2012. The reduction in the number of benefit entitlement errors overall was 26 percent.

b. Has the Acceptable Clinical Evidence Initiative contributed to the reduction of B2 errors? If so, how and what impact has it had?

Response. The Acceptable Clinical Evidence initiative is primarily intended as a convenience for Veterans and an efficiency tool for Veterans Health Administration clinicians. Because this is a relatively new initiative, more data is needed to assess the true impact.

Question 4. In discussing VA's appellate process, Under Secretary Hickey testified, "* * * we have a standard notice of disagreement form that will take 100 of those days immediately off that wait time for our veterans because we have never had a mandatory standard notice of disagreement form for an appeals before." What data does the Department rely upon that supports the assertion that use of a standard notice of disagreement form will reduce appeals processing time by 100 days?

Response. The Appeals Design Team Pilot, which ran from March 1, 2012, to March 1, 2013, found that control time was reduced to 7 days when using the standard notice of disagreement form. Control time for appeals processed outside of the pilot was 98 days during the same period. This represents a reduction of 91 days in the appeals process.

Chairman SANDERS. General Hickey, thank you very much for your presentation. I am going to begin my questions with the same question I asked in March when you were last before this Committee, and that is, the Secretary has set a very ambitious goal of processing claims within 125 days at 98 percent accuracy by 2015. That is a very, very ambitious goal.

According to this week's Monday Morning Workload Report, there were 693,857 pending claims, 57 percent or about 395,000 of which have been pending longer than the Department's goal of 125 days. These numbers clearly are better, significantly better than the last time we met and seem to indicate that VA is making very real progress.

My question to you is you have made progress, but you still have a long way to go. Do the Department's claim processing goals remain attainable? Are you, in fact, going to tell us this morning that you are on track to achieve the Secretary's goal of 125 days with 98 percent accuracy by 2015?

Ms. HICKEY. Chairman Sanders, we are on track. Barring any implications to our full Fiscal Year 2014 request, which we obviously need at the expiration of the continuing resolution in January, and barring any impact to our OIT budget, because we are particularly focused in 2014 on the automation that adds functionality every 12 weeks to our capability.

So, we will also require our full Fiscal Year 2014 IT budget when the CR expires in January of this year.

Chairman SANDERS. So, what you are telling us is that everything being equal, if you get the budget that you need, you expect to achieve the Secretary's goals?

Ms. HICKEY. That is what I am telling you, Chairman Sanders.

Chairman SANDERS. General Hickey, your testimony contains some significant statistics. It highlights a 36 percent reduction in the backlog since March of this year, including record numbers of claims completed in Fiscal Year 2013 and specifically the months of August and September, an improvement in claim level accuracy from 83 to 90 percent, and a continued conversion of millions of pieces of paper into a digital format suitable for use in the new electronic claims processing system.

Are you confident that VA will continue to see this level of production as well as continued improvement in accuracy?

Ms. HICKEY. Chairman Sanders, I am confident that we will continue to see that. I will say that we have achieved an historical high for VBA, never achieved before, which is 1.17 million claims in a single year, never done it before, never achieved 128,000 claims a month at the same time that our quality was also very high and rising, never achieved a 128,000 claim month.

Even November of this year where we achieved 94,000 claims, we have never achieved more than another month—74,000 claims. So, we are 20,000 high in the month of November, meaning 20,000 claims more have been produced in the month of November than we have ever done before, which is to show the demonstrated capabilities of where we are moving.

Chairman SANDERS. OK. Thank you. Let me just state that I have got a few more questions here.

In April of this year, VA rolled out an initiative to provide decisions on the claims that have been pending the longest. While I appreciate VA's efforts to provide the veterans who have been waiting the longest with decisions, I continue to have concerns about this initiative.

The IG, the Inspector General's recent findings regarding provisional ratings decisions at the Los Angeles Regional Office which found a number of errors was very, very concerning. I understand the office corrected the error by issuing appropriate guidance to staff in June and is now in the process of correcting any errors in claims which may have been improperly adjudicated.

So, this IG report is very concerning to many of us. Can you explain to this Committee any actions that have been taken to remedy the problems identified in Los Angeles?

Ms. HICKEY. Chairman, I absolutely can do that, but let me start first by saying the IG did go back and look at these claims later. But I will tell you the regional office knew within 1 week of doing this guidance they had misinterpreted the letter we sent. They were leaning in, trying to help to really move forward. No malicious intent. They put out an alternative guidance to the regional offices that they themselves identified within a week that they had done wrong.

The leadership at the regional office immediately notified Deputy Under Secretary Rubens of the issue. She immediately got in touch with everybody across the Nation, made sure no other guidance had been interpreted that way. It had not.

The regional office leadership immediately called not only one all-hands meeting to make sure everybody in the regional office knew they had made a mistake in the guidance, not the employees; but also then conducted a second all-hands meeting face-to-face with every employee to tell them about that and followed up with four more letters or written correspondence to the employees reminding them over periods of time about the guidance on this.

Now, it is important to note that this particular regional office had for the previous complete year made only one error like that in the whole year before. They had cut down those B2 errors that significantly. So, this was an anomaly.

Those claims that were looked at were found during that period of time and about the week after as it was still being cleaned up and trickled through.

So, yes, the IG did go in and identify them later, but the RO identified them immediately or within 1 week of making the wrong guidance decision.

It has been resolved. We had our star accuracy team pulling—and let me put it in context, this is 3 percent of those half a million or 14,000 or 512,000 claims we have made on the oldest claims initiative. We are reviewing every one of them to make sure it did not happen again. Our star accuracy through our compensation service is doing that.

Chairman SANDERS. OK. Thank you very much.

Senator Burr.

STATEMENT OF HON. RICHARD BURR, RANKING MEMBER, U.S. SENATOR FROM NORTH CAROLINA

Senator BURR. General, welcome to you and your team, and thank you for your testimony. Let me ask you, as it relates to the IG's report and the Los Angeles situation specifically, did the LA office violate VA policy in how they implemented that initially?

Ms. HICKEY. So, Senator Burr, yes, they gave out an alternative policy that they—they did not intend to violate policy. They just interpreted the policy differently.

Senator BURR. So, in that short period of time before they self-identified the misinterpretation of the memorandum, when they went back and reviewed all the provisional decisions, it found 470 out of 513. Can I assume that all 513 of those cases were decided in that 1 week period and those 470 errors were made in that 1-week period?

Ms. HICKEY. So, Senator Burr, I told you that we kept sending reminders. They had a second all-hands meeting and they had four more follow-ups because they found some of them were continuing to trickle out that way. So, it is about a 2–3-week period of time before they got the errors all caught and cleaned up, but they were actively and aggressively going after that cleanup.

Senator BURR. Were provisional decisions included in determining the number of claims VA is reporting it completed during 2013?

Ms. HICKEY. I am sorry, Senator, I am not understanding the question.

Senator BURR. Were provisional decisions included in determining the number of claims VA has completed during the calendar year 2013?

Ms. HICKEY. I am going to ask Ms. Rubens. She just told me yes. So I will answer yes on behalf of the Deputy Under Secretary. There were 14,000 of those claims which is 3 percent of all of the claims we have done in the oldest claim initiative, which was 67,000 at 2 years and older and 512,000 at 1 year and older.

Senator BURR. You highlighted 97 percent quality or accuracy. I will use both words. Last week The American Legion testified, "VA's accuracy statistics from the Monday Morning Reports are not consistent with the review of recently adjudicated claims as conducted by The American Legion." According to the Legion, they reviewed 260 decisions and found errors in 55 percent.

Also, the National Veterans Legal Service Program testified that the current error rate is somewhere between 30 and 40 percent. In some ROs it is higher. Are they wrong?

Ms. HICKEY. Senator Burr, it is an "apples and oranges" discussion; if I may have a moment to clarify. First of all, let me just state for the record and for every time I talk on this subject anywhere, we will not trade production for quality. It is an "and" equation. Both must rise, which is why it is 125 and 98.

But there is a very different way the IG and others look at issues than the way we do. I will tell you that our process has been validated by an external agency in——

Senator BURR. Let me ask my question again. Are they wrong?

Ms. HICKEY. Senator Burr, they are right for the way they look at it. We are right for the way we measure it, which is statistically valid.

Senator BURR. General, they are the customer, are they not?

Ms. HICKEY. Actually, the veteran, the family member, and their survivors are my customers, senator.

Senator BURR. Yes. And these are the organizations that represent them.

Ms. HICKEY. They are, sir, and they are our partners.

Senator BURR. Should this Committee believe that there is any VSO in America that believes that the accuracy or the quality is at 97 percent right now?

Ms. HICKEY. Senator Burr, I would ask you to ask them for their opinions. I can not quite——

Senator BURR. They testified on it. But that is not necessarily something that computes.

Ms. HICKEY. Senator Burr, I have a statistically valid, validated process that goes further——

Senator BURR. I asked a very simple question. Are they wrong? I guess the answer is yes because you are saying your statistics are different than what their review has been.

Ms. HICKEY. They have a different process, Senator.

Ms. HICKEY. OK. According to VA's Monday Morning Workload Reports, there are at least 266,000 appeals that have not been resolved. That is about 100,000 more than were pending 5 years ago. Although appeals are not counted in VA's backlog statistics, they represent individuals who have yet to know what benefits they received.

Do the performance standards for regional office directors and service center managers include how quickly and accurately they are handling appeals?

Ms. HICKEY. Senator Burr, the simple answer to your question is yes, they do; however, I would also tell you that a veteran does know the answer to our opinion on a claim. In many cases they are deriving resources associated with that claim decision already, even though they might be appealing only a part or piece of our overall decision.

Senator BURR. So, you have a metrics that you use to determine this?

Ms. HICKEY. We absolutely have metrics on our appeals, Senator.

Senator BURR. Would you provide that metrics for the Committee?

Ms. HICKEY. We will do that, sir.

RESPONSE TO REQUEST ARISING DURING THE HEARING BY HON. RICHARD BURR TO HON. ALLISON A. HICKEY, UNDER SECRETARY FOR BENEFITS, U.S. DEPARTMENT OF VETERANS AFFAIRS

Response. VBA establishes yearly performance standards to track regional office performance. Regional Office Directors are evaluated on the following appeals metrics:

• *Control time:* The number of days it takes to establish an appeal within VA systems
• *Pending appeals:* The number of appeals in the inventory
• *Average days pending:* The average length of time an appeal has been pending in the inventory
• *Average days pending for Form 9:* The average length of time a Form 9 (formal appeal) has been pending in the inventory
• *Avoidable remand rate:* The percent of remanded appeals that are remanded for an action that should have been taken by the RO prior to sending it to the Board.

As of January 31, 2014, approximately 72 percent of Veterans with pending appeals (318,000 Veterans) are receiving benefits.

Senator BURR. On average, how long have those 266,000 appeals been pending?

Ms. HICKEY. Senator, the Chairman cites some 800 days, and so I will accept——

Senator BURR. Does VA track that?

Ms. HICKEY. We do, Senator Burr.

Senator BURR. OK. At what point is an appeal considered to be backlogged?

Ms. HICKEY. We do not have a backlog number for appeals, Senator. What I can tell you is the rate of appeals has not changed in the last many decades.

Senator BURR. At what point does the length of an appeal become a concern to VA?

Ms. HICKEY. It is a concern of ours right this minute, sir. I will tell you that is why we have done a Lean Six Sigma effort on the appeals process to try to identify ways to improve the appeals process.

In fact, we have some legislation in front of you that I would appreciate your consideration to help the appeals process, and I appreciate the Members of this Committee who are supporting that.

I will also tell you we have a standard notice of disagreement form that will take 100 of those days immediately off that wait time for veterans because we have never had a mandatory standard notice of disagreement form for an appeals before, and that is, by the way, out for public comment right now. That period closes this month, and we hope to have that as soon as January 2014.

Senator BURR. Mr. Chairman, my last question in this round is, how many employees are currently devoted or dedicated to working on appeals?

Ms. HICKEY. Senator Burr, I can get you the specific number. I do not have that at my fingertips. But we have decision review officers who are dedicated in normal hours though they have been working overtime on compensation claims. They have been dedicated to working appeals.

Senator BURR. Would you provide that for the Committee and would you provide it in a way that you compare it to the previous 2 years and how many people were dedicated to appeals?

Ms. HICKEY. Senator, I would be happy to provide you what you need.

RESPONSE TO REQUEST ARISING DURING THE HEARING BY HON. RICHARD BURR TO HON. ALLISON A. HICKEY, UNDER SECRETARY FOR BENEFITS, U.S. DEPARTMENT OF VETERANS AFFAIRS

Response. VA appreciates Congress' investments in VBA and the Board of Veterans' Appeals to address appeals. While there is some variation in staffing levels throughout the year in all of our claims processing activities including appellate processing, VBA estimates that 899 and 902 full-time employees were dedicated to processing appeals in FY 2012 and FY 2013, respectively, including employees at the Appeals Management Center. Currently, 895 full-time employees are processing appeals in VBA. In the last two quarters of FY 2013, the Board hired and began training 100 new attorneys and increased the number of authorized Veterans Law Judges from 64 to 78. The Board currently has 628 employees processing appeals, a growth of approximately 22% in FY 2013.

Senator BURR. I thank the Chair.

Chairman SANDERS. Senator Burr, thank you very much.

Senator Brown.

Senator BROWN. So, why does it take 40 days longer in the Cleveland office?

Ms. HICKEY. Senator Brown, it depends on the amount of workload that the regional office has within its inventory. So, in some cases, we will have, as we have had in Ohio and as we have had in other locations, major demobilizations of large contingents of National Guard and Reserve that come back that create sudden surges in the system.

We have had that in Ohio. The Ohio National Guard has been participating very heavily in the current wartime environment so there have been some surges in returns as they redeployed.

Senator BROWN. But the backlog in Cleveland has been persistent for some time. Does not the VA need to respond? Why, if your community has sent more people to the National Guard, I guess that is what you are saying in part, so that you happen to live in a place where you have to wait 40 days longer is because you live in that place?

I understand if it is a surge and it is a short-term surge, but if it is persistent, is there not something VA should do to move people around or assist in a way that brings that a little more likely closer to the national average?

Ms. HICKEY. Senator Brown, there it is, and we have. So, let me just talk to you. Let me also say we had delivered yesterday to all of you—if you do not have it, please let us know. I will do Cleveland by example.

The inventory in Cleveland has been decreased by 47.2 percent over the last 8 months. The backlog is down by 64.5 percent. So, there is an improvement there.

Veterans in Ohio are now waiting less time for decisions. Almost 176.2 days less than they were waiting this time last year. Their 2-year-old claims, 99.1 percent of them are complete. Their 1-year-old claims, 73.4 percent of those are complete, and they have done it while increasing their quality 5 percentage points at the claim level and another 3.51 percent at the medical issue level.

But let me tell you how we did that. We did that by all-hands-on-deck—everybody in the Nation working on a national workload "queue" model that we have done over the last 8 months which helped all veterans regardless of State borders and have benefited from that help.

Senator BROWN. OK. Thank you.

Let me tell you a story. Sean Malone is a former Marine sergeant in New Vienna, Ohio. His claim had been pending in the development phase for 15 months. It appears the allegedly missing evidence that slowed his claim was already in the system but it was not routed to whoever is evaluating his claim.

It appears to me, and let me make sure I understand this, that there is a discrepancy. When there is a discrepancy between a claimant's status between paper mail and online—I understand it seems troublesome when requested evidence is missing or overdue.

My understanding is that there is no information provided online or in paper form about what evidence is outstanding, and there may be a discrepancy between the notification that there is evidence outstanding in paper format versus online.

Is that correct, and if it is, what do you do, what do we do to try to eliminate that discrepancy? In other words, whether you are filing online or are filing by paper, on paper, that one, you need to know that there is evidence missing whether it is online or paper; second, you need to know what specific evidence it is. It seems that we are falling short depending on how you file on either or both of those.

Ms. HICKEY. So, Senator Brown, I can absolutely both tell you what we are doing and what help we need.

Senator BROWN. OK.

Ms. HICKEY. This is an easier-to-do thing in IT and in automation: file to load that file directly onto that veteran's eBenefits account, but that takes a fully-funded IT budget in January when the CR expires.

IT for us is the way forward for really providing that even higher level of service to our veterans, their family members, and their survivors.

I will also say our VSOs who have met us online through the stakeholder enterprise portal will start to get that kind of information as well, but that also relies on a strong IT budget.

Senator BROWN. OK. Thank you, General.

Mr. Chairman, thank you.

Chairman SANDERS. Thank you, Senator Brown.

Senator Isakson.

Senator ISAKSON. General Hickey, what is a B2 error?

Ms. HICKEY. Senator, a B2 error is an examination error, either an insufficient exam or an exam where we asked for the wrong kind of exam, or a claim where we did not ask for an exam and we should have. That is a B2 error.

It had been, singularly prior to this year, our highest exam error, our highest error in general. But we put a big focus on it; we asked how do we go after the biggest error we make in the system. And I literally put it in all of our senior leaders' performance standards last year. I said you will reduce your B2 errors by 50 percent. Which they did.

Senator ISAKSON. What is it about the letter that you sent to the Los Angeles office that they misinterpreted that caused them to have a 91 percent error rate?

Ms. HICKEY. I would like to ask, since she has the very explicit language in the letter and had the conversation, I would like to defer that question to Ms. Diana Rubens, the Deputy Under Secretary for Field Operations.

Ms. RUBENS. Thank you, ma'am. Thank you, Senator Isakson.

Obviously, the Los Angeles Regional Office had a problem with B2 errors, as they interpreted the guidance that went out. It was, "do I have to wait for an exam that has been ordered or do I need to order an exam. The right answer, sir, was yes in both cases.

They misinterpreted that. Did not order exams when they should have. Obviously as soon as they discovered they had a spike in their B2 errors, they worked very quickly, as the Under Secretary has indicated, to correct that.

Ms. HICKEY. I will also add——

Senator ISAKSON. Excuse me. So, they misinterpreted and did not order an exam to justify a provisional decision. So, the error was they did not order the exam they should have ordered? Is that correct?

Ms. HICKEY. Senator, if I can answer that question. In many of those cases, they did order an exam but they made the decision before they got the exam results back. In other cases, they did not order the exam. But there is a mix of that.

Senator ISAKSON. Is there a particular medical problem that causes your adjudicators the biggest problems? Is there a particular medical condition?

Ms. HICKEY. So, we have put TBI at the top of the list for some of those medical conditions. I will tell you that is one of the things you do see in our IG reports because our IG is focused on that narrow subset of claims when they go out to look at us.

In fact, what I will tell you is in the testimony last week, they cited those errors but what I would like to tell you was in none of those errors cited was there at entitlement problem to the veteran. The veterans still got what the veteran deserved.

We made a process error where we did not get the second signature but not an outcome error. I will say I do appreciate it when the IG tells me we have a process where we have set a policy and we have people not doing what we said in policy.

Though in many cases, the errors that they call us on are not an outcome to the veteran problem. They are that we are not doing, what we have given out as policy in the process perspective, and that is what was reflected in the TBI condition.

But I do appreciate when they tell me that somebody is not following policy. That helps us clean that up.

Senator ISAKSON. Would it be fair to say that soft tissue determinations are the most difficult for VA to make a final determination on?

Ms. HICKEY. I cannot state that, Senator Isakson. I will go look to see if there is any data that sheds any light on that for us.

Senator ISAKSON. Well, my personal observation is that I think it would be because it is the most difficult assertation to make.

One other particular question. Has Secretary Petzel retired? I know he was getting ready to retire.

Ms. HICKEY. Senator, he has not yet but we have gone through the initial processes to begin the selection for his replacement.

Senator ISAKSON. Well, I just want to make one comment for you to deliver back to Secretary Shinseki and Mr. Petzel. We had a hearing in Atlanta in August 2012 on the veteran suicide problem at the Atlanta VA but also focused nationwide on the problem—that 22 veterans a day, 8000 a year are taking their own life—and in certain cases in the Atlanta VA, we found some holes in the follow-up on patients who came into VA and were followed up, were not followed up on in terms of their connecting with their counseling and their further appointments.

I want to thank VA for the attention they have been paying most recently to the veteran suicide issue but please remind them that until we get our arms around this we are going to continue to focus like a laser beam on that problem because it is the single biggest problem facing our veterans community today.

Ms. HICKEY. Senator Isakson, we will join you in focusing extremely hard on this issue. Even the loss of one life due to suicide is one too many.

Senator ISAKSON. Thank you very much.

Chairman SANDERS. Senator Isakson, thank you very much.

Senator Blumenthal.

Senator BLUMENTHAL. Thank you, Mr. Chairman.

I want to join Senator Isakson and commend him for raising this issue which is linked to another problem. Increasingly prevalent among our veteran community is the invisible wounds of Post Traumatic Stress often linked to suicide, unfortunately though not always.

I want to call attention to the effort that has been made with respect to veterans of previous wars, Vietnam and others before Iraq and Afghanistan, to qualify them for benefits because of Post Traumatic Stress, that they may have suffered with a condition that was unrecognized at the time, in fact, completely undiagnosed and untreated but very much a factor for them.

I know that there has been a settlement recently with respect to Mr. Shepherd of Connecticut whose claim was brought by the Yale Veteran Legal Clinic. My hope is that perhaps that recognition can become more general with respect to other veterans and I would like to ask for a report back, an update, as to what the status of consideration is in VA of Post Traumatic Stress and at the Department of Defense in terms of what veterans of previous wars have suffered.

Let me focus, though, on the appeals issue which has been raised here. Why does VA have no time measure for appeals? You mentioned that you do not keep track of—maybe I misunderstood your point there—but you do not have a metric on the time taken for appeals.

Ms. HICKEY. Senator Blumenthal, we absolutely have a metric down to every single area on the time it takes to do the appeals workload. What I said was we did not have a 125-days similar goal, or stretch goal as has been mentioned before.

If I can really quickly thank you for bringing up the PTSD issue because I would like to share on it. Our Secretary made a very effective decision to really enable many, many more serving members from all cohorts to have access to VA as a result of having PTSD.

By example, in 1990 we had 49,000 service veterans on our PTSD roles. In 2009 when the Secretary came, that number was 355,000. Today, it is over 750,000 people that we now are paying benefits to and now have access to different forms of health care in VA associated with PTSD.

The last thing I would just point out is, though it was not remarked in last weeks HVAC hearing, one of the three things that IG had been regularly looking at us for was the accuracy of our PTSD decisions.

They have recently informed me they are not seeing problems. So, therefore, they are going to discontinue looking.

Senator BLUMENTHAL. I want to come back to the appeals, if I may.

Ms. HICKEY. Yes, please.

Senator BLUMENTHAL. I stand corrected. In fact, I misspoke. I understand that you do measure the length of time for appeals and that you do not have the 125-day metric which would have been the more accurate way of putting it. But what I am troubled to find is that, unless I am wrong, the average length of appeals has actually increased by about 7 percent since March. Is that correct?

Ms. HICKEY. Senator, I do not have that metric specifically but what I can tell you is the rate of filing has not increased. In fact, it has been pretty steady——

Senator BLUMENTHAL. Well, what about the rate of decision?

Ms. HICKEY. It has not changed either.

Senator BLUMENTHAL. The average length of time?

Ms. HICKEY. Let me answer you by example. For the claim decisions we make in a year, about 11 percent of our veterans file what we call a Notice of Disagreement. At the end of a process that includes our regional offices, about 4 percent of those go forward to the Board of Veterans' Appeals. At the end of the Board of Veterans' Appeals process, about 1.2 percent or about 12,500 claims are overturned by the board who disagree with our decision in the claims process.

Senator BLUMENTHAL. Is at number increasing or diminishing?

Ms. HICKEY. Interestingly enough, it has held fairly constant in the last several decades. I will tell you I do not know what it means but this Fiscal Year 2013 is down.

Senator BLUMENTHAL. Can you get us the number, and I apologize for interrupting, but my time is expiring.

Ms. HICKEY. I understand.

Senator BLUMENTHAL. Could you get us the number for the length of time that is required for resolution of appeals? I understood it increased by 7 percent.

I would also like you to tell me why the percentage of backlog claims in the Hartford office has increased from 57 to 58.6 percent?

Ms. HICKEY. Senator, actually my data has something different. My data shows that your inventory in Hartford is down 9.1 percent; and your backlog is down 6.0 percent. The age of your claims is down 59.1 days right now. Your 2-year-old claims, you have none left in Hartford. Your 1-year-old claims, you only have very few, 18 of them remaining. Your quality is actually up 8.6 percentage points and your issue-based accuracy is up to 96.05 percent, a 1.73 percentage increase.

And that is while you also have been helping in the national workload.

Senator BLUMENTHAL. May I ask you what date that is?

Ms. HICKEY. This is as of November 30, 2013.

Senator BLUMENTHAL. I had data as of December 7 which is more recent data. It shows that the backlog has increased from 57 percent to 58 percent. I would like you to tell me why.

Ms. HICKEY. Senator Blumenthal, we will absolutely take that and try to explain that for you.

Senator BLUMENTHAL. Thank you.

Ms. HICKEY. You are welcome.

Chairman SANDERS. Thank you, Senator Blumenthal.

Senator Boozman, are you up? Or Senator Heller, I think is up next.

All right, Senator Heller.

Senator HELLER. Thank you. Thank you very much, Mr. Chairman and Ranking Member Burr, again for having this hearing. In my opening statement I said, General Hickey, that I believe that you knew this was a problem and you want to solve this problem and you are going to do everything you can to solve it. So, I appreciate that.

You have been giving some interesting statistics about Hartford and Cleveland. Can you give me the Reno statistics?

Ms. HICKEY. I absolutely can.

Senator HELLER. Thank you.

Ms. HICKEY. I will share them with you now.

Senator HELLER. Thank you.

Ms. HICKEY. We did have a big problem in Reno. I am pleased that we had an opportunity to address some of that problem, though we know we still have others to solve there.

Inventory is down by 42.1 percent. The backlog is down by 57.7 percent. The inventory, the age of the inventory they have in their system right now today remaining is 194.9 days younger than it was this time last year.

They have eliminated all but 13 of their 2-year-old claims for a 94.5 percent improvement. They have eliminated 90.9 percent of all their 1-year-old claims, and they have increased their claims space accuracy by 8.38 percent to over 92 percent, and their medical issue accuracy has been at 95 percent and remains at 95 percent.

Senator HELLER. Thank you. I guess my concern is have you had a chance to make it to the Reno RO. I know you have a lot of ROs.

Ms. HICKEY. I have actually been to Reno three times in 2 years and a few months.

Senator HELLER. You know, we always rank it as the worst RO. Can you give me any insight as to why that is the case and why we continue to be one of the worst?

Ms. HICKEY. Senator, this was not always a challenge for the Reno office. In fact, they have had times where they are on the top of the list. But they did have a growth of claims at a time where they had some vacant positions in the workforce, and simultaneously they had some retirements in the workforce. Between those kinds of numbers when you are a very small regional office, as Reno is, you see the impact pretty quickly.

Senator HELLER. You cited in some of your answers and I think a little bit in your opening statement about some of the concerns in surges that we have. My concern is that I think it is going to take maybe one major court decision or perhaps another military action to get us where we were a couple of years ago. I am not sure the structural changes are there.

We are looking at improvement, and I am glad to see that. But I know VA has cited a number of reasons as to why we got to where we were recently and that is obviously the changes to the diseases associated with Agent Orange.

Obviously, court cases that have expanded VA's duties—and frankly I think VA's own outreach and efforts—have increased claims also.

I guess what we are trying to hear in this Committee is how do we keep a surge from erasing perhaps all of these improvements that we have seen in the last year?

Ms. HICKEY. Thank you, Senator, for your questions; and I will reflect back to my DOD days if I might for a moment.

When we would go into a contingency operation, we did not go in with the resources we had. We went into that contingency operation with a supplemental that addressed the new requirements that that contingency brought to us that were outside of the planning environment.

I will tell you from the way we look at it, every time we get a new thing—you are right—I am telling you I will get to 2015 and 125 days except if I have a large perturbation of something like we experienced in the Agent Orange environment—260,000 claims in our inventory overnight in October 2010—that will kill us.

So, I cannot budget for a totally unknown, unprojected, inability-to-plan-for contingency operation that I do not know is coming, and that I have no idea will happen in a court case. But I do think in the future we ought to consider resources along with some of those new requirements. I think this needs to be addressed.

Senator HELLER. Thank you.

Mr. CHAIRMAN. Senator Heller, thank you very much.

Senator Boozman.

Senator BOOZMAN. Thank you, Mr. Chairman.

Again, we really do appreciate all your efforts. This is a difficult situation. I know you are working very hard.

I was in the veterans' benefit office or got to visit with them last week in the Little Rock area. You know, they have a good story to tell. They are working very, very hard. They mentioned the partnerships with the VSOs and our county veteran service officers, the great job that they were doing getting the pre-material ready so that they would have less problems.

I have a couple of things. The IG has not been real pleased in the sense you mentioned, you know, the key to this was the IT in the future. We struggled with that. We have had some problems.

Can you tell us, besides rolling out new versions, what is VA doing to remedy the issues in regard to that particular problem?

Ms. HICKEY. So, first——

Senator BOOZMAN [continuing]. Meaning, the benefits management system.

Ms. HICKEY. Thank you, Senator, I will address that.

First, let me just thank this Committee and specifically Senator Burr for your leadership around the fully-developed-claims process. That is tremendously good for our veterans and, frankly, it is tremendously good for us too and our ability to meet the needs of our veterans. You have provided an awesome tool to our VSOs who are just rolling in in big ways, including your county service officers, with more and more fully-developed claims.

So, I just want to acknowledge what you have done there in that leadership role. Now, our veterans get a whole year of additional benefits as a result.

Let me speak now to the VBMS system. I will tell you this time last year when we were deploying VBMS, we did have some latency issues. I spoke to you about that the last time. We had about three major issues with VBMS.

We rolled in hard. We are doing what the industry calls DevOps now which is when they put the developer with the operator, sitting side-by-side, fixing issues as we go, so that it works for the user and the coder knows what to code right the first time. I believe a lot of those issues were resolved with the January 2013 release that cleaned up a lot of those really big issues.

Do we have things that happen every now and then? Yes. I will tell you last week we had an access down time on VBMS, not because of VBMS. We had another underlying infrastructure that affected all of our systems.

So, that has been fixed, that has been resolved. It is not the system itself. It was the underlying hardware. There was a server somewhere that needed a new server.

But I will tell you we have it all backed up. And I will tell you frankly on that day the ingenuity of our employees said, "run to ground; find every paper claim we can find in the system that is left and start working those on the old legacy system." As a result, we still had a decent amount of production that day.

That is what I would tell you. I think VBMS is delivering every 12 weeks new and improved functionality.

I hear that from my employees sitting at the keys, banging it out, because I talk to them once a week on a pulse check call for 2–3 hours. Nobody else is allowed to do it.

I talk to bargaining unit employees only who are using the system and get to their challenges and their likes. They are telling me if you are a rater you really like it. If you are a VSR, there is still a little change management going on because I have built the checklist into the system that does not allow you to work around things and create errors. So, there is still some adjustment from our VSR's in that respect.

Senator BOOZMAN. Right. Tell me about what has happened to the non-rating actions, those claims. We focused a tremendous amount, rightly so, on the other but the dependency adjustments, changes to clothing allowance, things like that. What has happened to those claims?

Ms. HICKEY. I am happy to do so. I am trying to get to my page that gives me the explicit number but what I can tell you as I am flipping pages is that, in addition to having the all-time record-setting year for rating claims this year, I am happy to report that for the non-rating workload we also had the all-time historical record for those claims, doing more than 875,000 of those non-rating pieces. That is a 16 percent increase over last year.

Senator BOOZMAN. You mentioned to the Senator that was concerned about his statistics and you mentioned that his 2-year rate had gone down significantly.

How much of that would be provisional in regard to the category of over 2 years?

Ms. HICKEY. Probably very little when we have at most 14,000 claims across the Nation out of 512,000 claims.

Senator BOOZMAN. Thank you.

Ms. HICKEY. Thank you.

Chairman SANDERS. Senator Boozman, thank you very much.

General Hickey, I would be remiss, having heard your status reports from Connecticut, Ohio, and Nevada, to not ask you about Vermont. How are we doing in Vermont?

Ms. HICKEY. Mr. Chairman, I will tell you that White River Junction has decreased its inventory by 25 percent and has reduced its backlog by 34 percent.

The days that your veterans are waiting for their decisions, they have been reduced by 127 days. They are wading into today's inventory. They have completed 18.4 percent more claims this year than last year. They have no 2-year-old claims, those are 100 percent complete. And they have no 1-year-old claims, they are 100 percent complete, while they have also increased their quality at the claim level by 15 percentage points, almost 16 full percentage points in White River Junction, and their issue-based quality is up at 96 percent for a 4.25 percent increase.

Chairman SANDERS. OK. Thank you.

Let me raise very briefly two issues. I know that Senator Burr you have some questions you want to ask.

I want to talk a little bit about Web-based claims filing. I want to follow up on an issue I wrote the Secretary about last week and I appreciate both your and the Secretary's efforts to finally move VA into an electronic claims processing environment, something obviously long-overdue.

However, as VA continues its transition to a paperless environment, it needs to ensure that it does not inadvertently disadvantage certain populations of claimants. That is why I am so concerned about an ongoing transition of web-based claims filings from the veterans online application, VONAPP, to eBenefits.

At present, pension claimants can no longer file online as I understand it. This seems like a step in the wrong direction. The veterans with service prior to 1988 and no Defense Enrollment Eligibility Reporting System, or DEERS, identifier must physically visit a regional office before gaining the necessary access to file an application for disability compensation online. You, I think, can understand how difficult that may be for elderly veterans or those living in rural areas.

I would very much urge—I would make the same request of you that I made to the Secretary—first, will you restore VONAPP filings capabilities for pension applicants until such time as pension applications are available in eBenefits?

Ms. HICKEY. Mr. Chairman, I will take this one. We own this one. I did see your letter. We are responding to your letter but let me just give you the elevator response here.

The VONAPP capability still exists; however, it is on our pension page. Now, we have not, and I own this, done a very good job about telling our veterans that is where it is.

So, we will take that for action and we will get the message out there better and faster so those applicants can still use some of that capability.

Second, just as I say to every veteran, I will say it again today, I think one of the best ways to navigate our system is to get a certified VSO, State, county, Federal, local somebody to help. I really do value that they give it——

Chairman SANDERS. I know that but not every veteran has access.

Ms. HICKEY. Absolutely, I understand that.

What I will tell you is that we have built something called the 527EZ for our veterans. It is the counterpart to the 526EZ online form on eBenefits. That will be loaded eventually into eBenefits. It depends on IT dollars.

What I can also tell you that I hope will help is, and I have seen this—I was helping a veteran myself on this—when you go in for an eBenefits account, if you are one of those veterans who do not show up in the DEER system, there is some functionality on the bottom of that page. We need to do a better job of highlighting it which I will take that for action.

But if you click on that and say, I am having a problem, it goes to three people at our benefits assistance service who are dedicated to getting you in the system. We need to do a better job about getting that word out.

Chairman SANDERS. Not everybody is as familiar with IT as you are.

Ms. HICKEY. I understand, Mr. Chairman. Thank you. We will do a better job about getting that word out across the system.

Chairman SANDERS. I think my last comment is that you have heard a lot of concern this morning about the appeals process. We are concerned about the rise in the appellate workload pending at the regional offices.

The average amount of time it takes to resolve an appeal which, according to VA's performance and accountability report was 866 days in 2012, is clearly unacceptable. So, what I want to hear from you is how, with very specific ideas, we are going to improve the processing of the appellate workload, and I would very much like to hear from you within 45 days, by your telling this Committee the actions VBA will take to improve the processing of the appellate workload at the regional offices.

Can I have your commitment on that?

Ms. HICKEY. Mr. Chairman, yes, you can and I would be happy to deliver that.

Chairman SANDERS. Thank you very much.

Senator Burr.

Senator BURR. I thank the Chairman.

General Hickey, thank you for your comments as it relates to fully develop claims. I think the Committee has always tried to provide anything that they thought might make the system better. I think it is good to know that that is having an impact.

Let me reiterate to you and your team anything, and I say anything, that the Committee can do from a legislative standpoint that makes the situation better we are anxious to hear those requests. I would hate for this hearing to go on without us not reiterating that one more time.

In your conversation with Senator Boozman as it related to the VBMS, I have got a follow-up because last week the Inspector General testified that claims processing staff had complained that the VBMS system has, "spontaneous system shutdowns, latency issues related to slow time to develop documents such as medical evidence for review, longer times to review electronic evidence, mislabeled electronic evidence, and mixing evidence from one veteran's electronic file to another veteran's file."

Is that an accurate depiction by the Inspector General?

Ms. HICKEY. Senator Burr, I think it may be a very dated perception by the Inspector General.

Senator BURR. Have you heard similar complaints from employees?

Ms. HICKEY. Senator, a year ago I may have heard similar comments from employees which I listened to every single week. We did have latency issues last year. We did have some issues in the system. We do not have the same issues in the system.

But if I can couch that really quickly, there is some change management that has to happen in this, as well. When you are doing something electronic, you are standing there looking at the screen the whole time. You forget about how much time you had to waste when it was in paper. You had to go upstairs two flights, go find the file in the file bank, pull the file out of the file bank, run downstairs, go to the mail room, find the associated mail that was hanging around in paper, bring it back, go to the copier, go get the sticky 3M notes, write it all down.

You sort of forget about all that logistical time that you used to spend. So, suddenly 3–20 seconds feels like a big deal when you are standing looking at a screen doing nothing.

Senator BURR. But you are actively involved in a weekly conversation on the phone and you are not hearing any of this?

Ms. HICKEY. I am. I hear occasionally now, I heard it a lot last November. So, I will acknowledge that. I heard it a lot last November, while I had the IT guys sitting there with me, and the VBMS program management office sitting there with me, and we are asking them literally for the note that they sent in to the national help desk on it. We are looking at exactly the right time and what happened and how it needed to be fixed.

Senator BURR. OK. We will follow up with the IG to see the timeliness of what he reported in his testimony.

Ms. HICKEY. Thank you, Senator.

Senator BURR. The Monday Morning Reports also reflect there has been an increase in the number of days, the number of work items pending in categories like correspondence, miscellaneous determinations, and dependency adjustments and that these have been increases that have been pending for a long time.

For example, the number of dependency adjustments increased from 48,000 in 2010 to 228,000 today and 71 percent have been pending more than 125 days compared to 19 percent in 2010.

Let me just be blunt. Has VA been putting off this type of work in order to focus resources on driving down the backlog numbers?

Ms. HICKEY. As equally responsive to you, Senator Burr, no. It is indicative by the fact that we have done an all-time record high number of those, 875,000 of them and we are 16 percent more productive this last year over the previous year.

So no, we are not putting them off but I have good news to tell you——

Senator BURR. So, why are these piling up?

Ms. HICKEY. Because we are doing more claims, Senator. As we do more claims, we get more dependency claims. As you all have told me, and I accept that, as we have been slow, you have sent more letters, rightfully so, that we need to acknowledge and respond to at the local level so I will acknowledge that.

I am trying hard to get that mail volume down for you by doing that claim right and well for our veterans and their family members and survivors, I acknowledge there are a lot of letters that have grown over this time.

But what I will tell you, we do have a really good solution set to talk to you about, and I think non-rating workload is perfect for automation. It does not have an adjudicative, judgmental, non-objective rule set associated with it.

We have just built this last year, something called RVPS, focused at dependency claims. When you file a claim online on eBenefits today for dependents, 40 percent of them go through in a single day and pay. This week we are loading another set of functionality focused at our retiree population. It will take 60 to 70 of those, flow them through in a single day—automated, done and moving out.

I think this non-rating workload is really, really conducive to automated IT solutions. That is where we are focused for this next year.

Senator BURR. Ms. Rubens, VA's testimony mentions generation three of the VBMS and that it will deploy next year with additional capabilities including a national queue, "will route claims automatically based on VBA's priorities." I think that is in large measure what you were just talking about, General.

It says that the processor will place the claim with the next best person to work based upon the skill level and national policy.

Is VBA working on a national policy?

Ms. RUBENS. Thank you, Senator Burr.

The effort behind the national work queue really is to take things like our Priority 1 claims today—our Congressional Medal of Honor recipients, our former POWs, the category, if you will, of the homeless veteran, the terminal, the hardship—that is, of course, our first priority.

Then as we continue to work the aged claims down, we started with the over two category, then 1 year, and now we are all on the 334-day bucket. Those are the kinds of policies that the national work queue will help with to make sure that those claims get routed properly, whether that is to a member of an express lane, a core lane, or a special operations lane depending on the nature of the claim to ensure we are, if you will, managing that as efficiently as possible.

Senator BURR. Am I just misinterpreting the statement that? I understand the part about routing the claim the most appropriate place regardless of geographically where that is. Is there an over-arching national policy that exists on top of that? Or is that routing national policy?

Ms. HICKEY. Well, Senator Burr, those categories that she just mentioned including, by the way, we put fully developed claims in that because we want to incentivize folks to bring us in a fully developed claim.

The national policy is just saying what is the workload we want you to do first. So, we do not want you to go grab something easy off the list and off the shelf just because it is easy for you to do. We want you to do the things we say nationally are critically important for us to do to get to 125–98.

Senator BURR. My question earlier was, what participation did critical stakeholders have in the development of that national policy?

Ms. HICKEY. Well, I personally engage monthly with the executive directors of all of the VSOs and also monthly with all of the executive directors from the military support offices, the MSOs, as well.

We go over every single initiative we are doing, every single strategy they do.

Senator BURR. Do they contribute to the development of that national policy?

Ms. HICKEY. They do. They give us input. They say where they think we should do something differently. We change and address and adapt in that environment as well. I completely ran the old claims initiative through and by them. In fact, I think we called a special meeting just before that.

Senator BURR. Last, if I can——

Chairman SANDERS. I have got to run. Senator Burr will take over.

I want to thank all of you for being here. It is very clear to me that we are making significant progress. It is also clear to me that there are a lot of problems that remain. This Committee looks forward to working with you. Thank you.

Ms. HICKEY. Thank you, Chairman.

Senator BURR [presiding]. Thank you, Mr. Chairman.

General, VBMS 6.0 is scheduled to be released this month which includes delivering initial capabilities to the Board of Veterans' Appeals.

As we continue to see a decrease in the number of backlogged claims, it appears we can also expect to see the number of appeals increase. As VBMS is deployed to the board, it is critical that it does not hamper their ability to adjudicate appeals in a timely fashion.

The functions and requirements of regional offices and boards are significantly different. What steps has VBA and the Office of Information Technology taken to tailor-make the VBMS system to meet the need of the Board of Appeals?

Ms. HICKEY. Senator, great questions. I will tell you that from the get-go the board has been part of the requirements development process and, frankly, has driven the requirements development process because it is, in large part—at the end of the day we are building that functionality out for them and releasing them in this version.

We will add functionality just as we do every 12 weeks for the claims side. We will add functionality over time for the appeals side as well, but we will not do that in a vacuum.

In fact, I have to take the lead off of them for building out of their requirements.

Senator BURR. Great. Well, let me reiterated what the Chairman said. We are grateful to you for the job you do. Thank you for being here today.

General, if there is one take away I would at the conclusion of this emphasize with you, this inconsistency between what some of the VSOs perceive of the quality debate and what your numbers show the quality to be is something I hope you will focus on as to how we close the gap.

Both cannot be right; both cannot be wrong. I think that it is important that we all work off of the same metrics. I have asked you to share some metrics with us, and I hope you will get that here in a timely fashion.

By the same standpoint, we both know we still have got work to do and I want your team to know that the Committee is a willing partner to try to accelerate that in any way, shape, or form that we can, but not to sacrifice quality. I think we are all in agreement with that.

Ms. HICKEY. We are absolutely in agreement with that, Senator.

Senator BURR. We thank you for your time.

This hearing is adjourned.

[Whereupon, at 11:44 a.m., the Committee was adjourned.]

APPENDIX

PREPARED STATEMENT OF PARALYZED VETERANS OF AMERICA

Chairman Sanders, Ranking Member Burr, and Members of the Committee, Paralyzed Veterans of America (PVA) would like to thank you for the opportunity to offer our views on the VA's transformational progress, in particular, our views on the adjudication of VA's most complex disability claims to ensure quality, accuracy and consistency on these complicated issues. PVA has a unique expertise in dealing with complex claims because our members have complex disabilities as a result of spinal cord injury or dysfunction.

The Department of Veterans Affairs (VA) has fully deployed its new processing model for disability compensation claims, called the Veterans Benefits Management System (VBMS), in order to reduce the number of backlogged claims. This paperless processing model places an emphasis on expediting claims where the supporting documentation is fully developed by the Veteran. But the success of VBMS greatly depends on the process design, like rules-based processes, and supportive technologies like Special Monthly Compensation (SMC) calculators, that undergird the system.

Unfortunately, rules-based systems treat all veterans the same and can be flawed by imperfect rulemaking and application, invariably leading to increased errors for these claims. This is the challenge for a rules-based computer system; it does not have the human interaction to fully understand the circumstances of a specific injury. The numerous issues faced by veterans with catastrophic injuries create a complex set of outcomes that cannot be easily reconciled by logic-based systems that cannot appreciate nuance in disability assessments. Calculators used in rules-based systems historically fail to compute the right ratings for persons with multiple issues. This type of decision analysis uses decision trees that attempt to enable the rater to simplify and resolve complex questions. This technique, however, can be problematic when the analysis involves highly qualitative assessments that are reduced to binary choices.

This processing model also handles claims for veterans who have unique circumstances, such as financial hardship, homelessness, or serious injuries or disabilities in special "segmented lanes." The problem is the growth in the number of claims considered "complex" since September 11, 2001. Complex claims, according to VA, are characterized by the number of issues per claimant filed, which has doubled to 8.5, when compared with claims from past wartime eras. Also of significance, of the 47,814 complex claims currently in the VA inventory, over half are backlogged. In fairness, this number has steadily decreased over time. But VA still takes too long to adjudicate these claims in many cases, particularly for our members with Amytrophic Lateral Sclerosis (ALS or Lou Gehrig's disease).

PVA has developed unique expertise in dealing with complex claims because our membership is predicated on having one of the most complex disabilities an individual can have: spinal cord dysfunction, whether due to injury or disease. This can occur due to trauma, ALS, Multiple Sclerosis (MS), and other debilitating causes, and often manifests in both primary and secondary residual losses throughout the bodily systems, including the often under-regarded "invisible" aspects of injury like mental impairment, need for attendant care, and helplessness. Complex claims in this regard go beyond the mere number of issues.

Accurately rating these losses for claim purposes requires expertise in neurology, physiatry, urology, psychiatry, and other specialty areas. But during Compensation & Pension (C&P) examinations, it is common to see a general practitioner authoring medical opinions on etiology, nature and extent of dysfunction and cumulative effect of separate yet concurrent disabilities. This is not a problem when the examiner devotes enough time to understanding the disability and its nuances before rendering a conclusion. However, this is not always the case. As a result, when these opinions result in lower ratings than the veteran should have received, the ensuing debate takes on a subjective hue when the regulations alone do not persuade a decision reversal.

While VBA has instituted an evaluation system that assigns greater weight to complex claims, these claims are often too esoteric for journeyman raters, full of embedded issues and ambiguities both legal and medical that lead to errors. Moreover, these issues do not lend themselves exclusively to rules-based analysis without inductive, common sense reasoning in many cases, such as reasonable doubt provisions, which seems to have slowly disappeared from training and guidance for new raters. Working these cases requires a combination of experience and open-mindedness to make a correct determination. And while a VA claim of 90 percent accuracy could be accepted, it is completely possible that this average is due to 99 percent accuracy on simple claims and 50 percent accuracy on complex claims. This possibility is not very comforting to those with complex claims.

For example, in one PVA case a veteran with ALS submitted evidence supporting a higher rating for Special Monthly Compensation at the R–2 rate from his treating physician, thus verifying his need for skilled care in his home. Despite substantiating his need with credible medical documentation, he had to subsequently submit to a C&P exam at the VA's direction where the examiner concluded he did not need skilled care on a daily basis because he had some limited movement. Not only did the examiner improperly contemplate movement as a basis for determining need for care, VA misapplied its own regulation on resolving doubt when two expert opinions conflict. When common sense is applied, there is little doubt on the question of whether a veteran with ALS, an incurable, quickly debilitating condition with foreseeable, inevitable consequences, needs skilled care. This case out of the San Diego VA Regional Office illustrates what happens when a profoundly complicated set of disabilities, a lack of expertise, subjective interpretation of regulations, and rules that do not allow for a "common sense override" option collide in a veteran's claim. In this instance, the veteran presented enough evidence from his VA clinician, yet VA still required a VA examination per inflexible VA guidance in such cases (see M21–1MR Part IV, Subpart ii, Chapter 2, section H). While PVA commends the Veterans Benefits Administration (VBA) for implementing such initiatives as the Acceptable Clinical Evidence option, which allows a rater to decide based on the record in lieu of a C&P exam, this has not taken root system-wide and this needs to be disseminated nationwide.

It would also help to eliminate redundancies such as unnecessary C&P exams that either corroborate the evidence of record or create arbitrary bases for denying a claim. PVA has long criticized VA's overuse of C&P examinations particularly when the evidence of record already substantiates the claim. These exams attempt to provide a snapshot of complex disabilities based on cursory review of the medical history and templates, called Disability Benefits Questionnaires (DBQs), that ask a lot of questions but not always the right ones. For example, "need for higher level of assistance" is not asked on the ALS DBQ, even though the terminal nature of the disease makes constant need for specialized care likely in virtually every case. And with the addition of rules-based calculators that make C&P exams a mandatory step in many instances, these incorrect decisions are given the patina of unassailable faultlessness. PVA is on record stating that rules-based calculators and processing are not conducive to accurate analysis where complex claims, as we describe them, are concerned. They can be adequate starting points. But these claims require experienced raters who, for example, would not conclude that a veteran who can barely stand up due to lost "useful" function should be rated the same as a veteran who can walk but with difficulty. Or that a veteran with paraplegia cannot be considered in need of aid and attendance because he manages his neurogenic bowel and bladder and dresses independently thus no longer being functionally disabled.

Experienced raters, not algorithms, best factor in the nuances of Special Monthly Compensation and areas of subjective interpretation that can lead to an incorrect decision. For this reason, PVA has previously asserted in testimony before the House and Senate Committees on Veterans' Affairs that reducing the backlog through the use of technologies cannot come at the expense of accurately rating the most complicated claims in the inventory. This is why PVA trained its service officers to fully develop a claim long before VA idealized the Fully Developed Claim concept. Our service officers know what questions to pose to an examiner, how to reconcile the medical and legal ambiguities, and how to draw a path toward entitlement for the rater from the time the claim is filed. But not every rater, particularly the new ones, can or feel empowered to see past the inflexible rules and seemingly indisputable C&P examinations enough to question or deviate when necessary.

Perhaps that is how it has to be in the grand scheme of the entire backlog and we understand that rules are critical to organizational success. But the exceptions are the rule for PVA. A veteran with ALS died in hospice while his claim was pending before a "Special Ops" lane coach because he needed a DBQ despite the fact that the evidence of record supported entitlement. A utilitarian system that successfully delivers benefits to one million veterans, but overlooks the most vulnerable, is inconsistent with the moral obligation derived from Lincoln's promise to those who served our country. As VA celebrates the success in reducing the backlog through the use of new technologies and innovative processes, more attention now needs to shift toward developing strategies for adjudicating complex claims more timely and accurately.

PVA believes there are several things that can be done to improve support to veterans needing SMC:

• SMC cases should be assigned only to the most experienced raters and VA must ensure that new raters are properly trained on SMC and its applicable regulatory doctrines.

• VA needs to allow for the application of a "common sense" override when rules-based processes limit or preclude necessary subjective analysis such as reasonable doubt or the weight/credibility of evidence, or fail to reconcile ambiguities in the medical evidence or legal applications

• It is critical that if denial of a complex claim is predicated on a C&P exam, particularly in cases of terminal illness or catastrophic disability, the reasons and bases must detail how the weight of all evidence was assigned, whether reasonable doubt applied or not, and whether the acceptable clinical evidence option was considered in lieu of ordering a C&P exam.

• VA must expand acceptable clinical evidence (VHA Directive 2012–025) for nationwide implementation.

• And finally, VA must ensure the rules-based process allows for and encourages the application of 38 CFR § 3.102, which defines "Reasonable doubt" doctrine. Accordingly, "When, after careful consideration of all procurable and assembled data, a reasonable doubt arises regarding service origin, the degree of disability, or any other point, such doubt will be resolved in favor of the claimant. Reasonable doubt means one which exists because of an approximate balance of positive and negative evidence which does not satisfactorily prove or disprove the claim." (Authority: 38 U.S.C. 501(a))

Historically, due to the nature of our catastrophically disabled membership, PVA has been the subject matter expert for claims involving multiple injuries or conditions. PVA has enjoyed the privilege of providing VA with help in field studies and advice on processes that best meet the unique needs of veterans with catastrophic injuries. PVA National Service Officers have even participated in the training of VA claims processors. This valuable service has tremendously benefited both organizations and illustrates an important, enduring partnership. PVA's success in claims processing is due to diligence in training our service officers and in understanding the challenges faced by those with the most complex of cases. VA must do the same. Data processing is no substitute for education, training and understanding. We fear that as VA continues to aggressively look to reduce the backlog, complex claims may move further behind. While advances have been made in processing theses claims for those most needing, we caution the Committee and VA not to become too satisfied with successes that are achieved now while some veterans are still left behind. PVA looks forward to continuing to make VA aware of the need to keep complex claims in the forefront and to ensure they are properly and quickly adjudicated, particularly as they impact our most catastrophically injured veterans.

We thank you for the opportunity to submit our views for the record and we would be happy to answer any questions you may have for the record.

○